The Hour
of
The Helicopter

K. D. BELDEN

FIRST PUBLISHED 1992 BY
LINDEN HALL
223, PRESTON ROAD, YEOVIL
SOMERSET, BA20 2EW

© K. D. BELDEN
ISBN 0 948747 10 2

COVER DESIGN BY W. CAMERON JOHNSON

PHOTOTYPESET BY INTYPE, LONDON
PRINTED IN ENGLAND BY
BIDDLES LTD., GUILDFORD, SURREY

Contents

FOREWORD BY HILARY AND DAVID BELDEN ... ix

PREFACE ... xii

1 "HOW VERY UNUSUAL" ... 1

2 YOU NEVER KNOW WHERE LIGHTNING WILL STRIKE ... 11

3 "I CALL YOU FRIENDS" ... 27

4 SECRET OF TEAMWORK ... 37

5 THE HOUR OF THE HELICOPTER ... 46

6 FISHERS OF MEN ... 56

7 HUSBAND AND WIFE ARE ONE . . . ? ... 67

8 PILGRIMS OF THE IMPOSSIBLE ... 87

9 THE CREATIVE DECADE ... 107

10 "FOUNTAINS OF FELICITY" ... 116

11 REMAKERS OF THE WORLD? ... 130

12 "GREET THE UNSEEN WITH A CHEER" ... 143

For Stella
loved companion of the way
and for
Hilary, David, Deborah
and Rowan

Foreword

WE ARE delighted that Dad has written this story.

Of course, in some sense, it is also our own.

We were brought up on an unexpected mixture: printer's ink and good cooking, prayer and London's theatre world, free school meals and a posh Mayfair address.

Dad, we realised as we grew up, could have led a very different life. He might have been a professor of medieval history, poring over manuscripts, or raising the money for the college's new wing and spreading his characteristic warmth beyond the college walls.

He could clearly have been successful in business: with his organising skills and drive, his ability to inspire and to visualise the whole picture and the details simultaneously.

But he is also an artist: his appreciation of colour and design and his own paintings helped form our idea of beauty. He enjoys a mixture of simple shapes in complex relationships and clear, vivid colours – as in the orderly riot of Provençal roofs he painted in the Fifties – peaceful and alive.

As a young man, he found, through the Oxford Group, his calling to love and serve God. His life and his many talents have been devoted – with humour, warmth and commitment – to that calling and that growing fellowship.

Our small nuclear family comes from a background of Norfolk weavers and farmers, Channel Island builders and the odd portrait painter or shopkeeper. In our home, we met people from all over the world. We can remember sharing meals with a West African Chief or a senior BBC journalist, with trades union leaders or actors or au pair girls, with Hindu students or Muslim politicians.

We learnt, as we lived with them, to call an unusually large number of people our friends and family – we were grown-up before we celebrated Christmas with fewer than twenty round the table. This Christmas group, incidentally, always included our two older, eccentric, maternal uncles who deeply disapproved of MRA and a life lived on 'faith and prayer' rather than a proper salary and career but who loved Mum and Dad and us and were intrigued by our 'family'.

In the midst of the work our parents and 'extended family' were doing, we went to school and came home, had our pets (a series of hamsters) and our toys and hobbies; we sat exams, went cross-country running; we were mad about rock 'n roll and the theatre. We sometimes tolerated, sometimes supported, sometimes opposed or resented their particular brand of active Christian life. The children of clergy, of politicians, of anyone with a cause or an all-consuming job will understand our mixed reactions.

What we both recognise is the love and commitment Mum and Dad have shown: to Christ, to each other and to us – and then to the much wider family into which they have welcomed everyone. That model of welcome has been a good one for school management or for communes and cooperatives. They link it with a penetrating realism about the difficulties, however good the cause, which people have in living and working honestly and lovingly with each other. There was a strong spice of drama, disagreement and humour throughout our childhood.

Both of us have taken the vision and reinterpreted it outside the particular framework of MRA – but any true vision should continually inspire not sameness but variety, change and growth, hope and joy for the future in a suffering world.

Dad has written this book to present some of the experiences and insights of this unexpected life. His old friend, Denis Foss, has published it. The book's publication comes from us to Mum and Dad with love.

We hope you will also enjoy it.

Hilary and David Belden

Preface

THIS is not an autobiography – more a kind of travelogue, with comments along the way on some of the experiences that have gone into trying to find and follow the road of faith. Such a search often seems to be less like climbing a mountain with a load on your back than like stepping into a helicopter and being lifted to a new level of living. As St. Paul tells us, "He lifts us right out of the old life". And this often comes from spending enough time before God, especially in that morning hour before the rush of the day begins.

But following these experiences of "lift-off" the journey still has to be made, and there are many lessons to learn or re-learn as time goes on. This book tries to share some of these as they have come at different stages over a lifetime.

Everyone's life has its rugged patches, and none of us is immune, but for my part the gains far outweigh the hard parts. I am filled with gratitude for our family, for our calling, for a host of friends across the world. Some years ago my wife and I were away from England for nine months, travelling in Africa – Ethiopia and Kenya, in Asia – India, Sri Lanka, Malaysia, Hong Kong, and in the Pacific – Papua New Guinea, Australia, New Zealand. In all those months we only spent three nights in a hotel (as someone's guests). Every other night was spent with friends in their homes, and we moved on the deepest levels of friendship wherever we went, united in the bond of our calling. Everywhere we found them at grips with the men and women who could affect the pressing issues in their countries.

We have seen and enjoyed so many memorable things, from the penguins marching in from the sea, dead on time, in Port Philip Bay in Australia to the Taj Mahal in India, so far exceeding any description; from the Golden Gate bridge in San Francisco over which we drove to our son and daughter-in-law's wedding, to the golden hills and snow-capped mountains of New Zealand. And those exquisite African dawns by Lake Naivasha in the Rift Valley, where we stayed with our friends Wilfred and Mairo Hopcraft: silver sky and silver lake, with the floating islands of papyrus and the giant Goliath heron, six feet high, waiting on one leg to catch his breakfast every morning, and then flapping away down the lake like a grand piano in flight. But this is not that kind of travelogue and I just mention these things to show that many delights have attended the travels we have been called on to make. I am the kind of person who much prefers to stay at home rather than travel anywhere, but that has not been our lot and portion!

The views expressed in this book are, of course, my own, though many of the experiences I have recalled come from more than half a century's active participation in the Oxford Group and its work of Moral Re-Armament. For many, like myself, the

Oxford Group has been a school of reality, a call to commitment and a vision of the world as our Creator would have it be.

Anyone who looks at the world today and sees the evidence of moral chaos and spiritual starvation, can hardly doubt the need for massive, world-wide moral and spiritual re-armament. Now events in Eastern Europe underline the human devastation caused by doctrines of unrelieved materialism, while the level of materialism in our Western democracies also causes mounting concern.

The issue is: can the world be set on a new course by anything less than a revolution in people – in their aims and motives, hopes, fears and hates? And can this come about through any lesser agency than the power of the living God? And isn't this the basic task we are meant to be engaged in?

1
"How very unusual"

"WHAT exactly is the Trinity?" I asked my mother, at the ripe age of five. Mother, who was a luminously sincere Christian but no theologian, was hard put to it to reply, and my response to her attempt is unrecorded.

Thirty five years later, at the same age, by an unexpected coincidence, my son David asked the same question of his mother. When my wife (who had read for a diploma in theology) had explained as best she might, his perceptive comment was, "How very unusual".

My father, who preached his last sermon a month before he died in his eighties and listened to his latest broadcast on the last morning of his life, is said to have preached his first sermon at the age of nine.

But it would be unwise to deduce from this precocious evidence that there is any strain of natural piety in the men of our family. Quite the reverse, in fact. A strain of natural curiosity would be nearer the mark. But this enquiry of mine, made during the First World War, seems as good a starting point as any for the journey which took me through childhood faith into agnosticism and atheism and, after a lapse of years and wholly unexpectedly, into faith again, but faith rooted now in experience, and maturing through the years.

I wish I could picture my parents to you. They were both born in the 1880's, my father a few years older and my mother a few inches taller, and they shared a graciousness from their upbringing which today seems indeed to come from another age.

Their meeting was improbable and unforeseeable, except, perhaps to the beneficent Intelligence Who arranges such things. In the early years of the century my mother lived with her parents in Ramsgate, over the men's wear shop in the High Street which my grandfather managed. James Richman and Edith Hunter had two daughters, Doris, my mother and her sister, Clarice. They were a devoted family. They were also active Christians. My grandfather, always impeccably dressed, with his neat imperial, his flashing eye and a great sense of humour, ran missions on the sands at Ramsgate in which his daughters were mobilised from an early age – Doris to play and Clarice to sing. My mother was a pianist and a painter, and in 1908, when she was just twenty-one, she was starting her career in teaching.

My father at this time was at his theological college, New College, London, on the splendid Swiss Cottage site long since replaced by modern buildings.

The Beldens were Norwich weavers who turned, like the rest of Norwich, to shoe-manufacturing in the mid-nineteenth century, after weaving moved to Yorkshire during the industrial revolution. My Belden grandfather was a last-maker and came to London in the 1870s to seek his fortune. He became a manufacturer in quite a big way, with a factory in the Great Dover Road. He sold his exquisitely turned lasts on the continent as well, especially in Germany.

His problem was the succession to the business. His elder son had emigrated to Canada, and all his hopes were centred on my father to take over. But my father, due perhaps to the influence of his Welsh mother, had a clear and compelling call to the ministry.

This led to considerable friction, and at one time my father was working in the factory and taking his theological degree at the same time. It nearly ruined his health. He used to fall asleep, he told me once, on a heap of shavings behind the machines, exhausted. One day he was walking up Richmond Hill and collapsed on the pavement. Passers-by carried him into a nearby chemist's shop and laid him out on the floor. The chemist, a kindly man who thought he was dying, put his arms under my father's head and said, "Remember, underneath are the everlasting arms." This reached father through the mists and he thought to himself, "Why, so they are!" At which he came to, got up, thanked the man, and walked out of the shop and went on his way. In later years his health became indestructible, but in those years it was precarious.

It was my Richman grandfather's practice to take his daughters from time to time for a short holiday to Westerham, in Kent. One weekend in 1908 he took Doris there. As usual, they went together to the little Congregational church. The service that day was being taken by a student preacher – my father, who was in his last year at college. They were moved by what he said, and spoke to him afterwards to thank him. They were also struck by how pale and ill he looked, and out of the kindness of his heart my grandfather impulsively asked him down to Ramsgate to stay with them for a week of sea air. He accepted. At the end of the week father, who was never one to hang back once his mind was made up, proposed to Doris.

Consternation broke out in the Richman family. Their precious daughter proposed to by this seedy theological student who hadn't yet got a church and probably wouldn't live long! They set about stopping it in the one way that was bound to make it happen: they forbade Doris and David to see each other or communicate in any way for six months. Then they would see if there was anything in it or not. The following April they were married and moved into the manse in Banbury, where my father had been called to his first church, and where I was duly born.

Forgive this rather lengthy background. It goes some way to explain how it was that I grew up, so to speak, on the inside of religion, and yet in an atmosphere which was also adventurous and unconventional, however clearly drawn the moral lines might be.

Being the minister's son put me in a somewhat privileged position, and one which had nothing to do with class and everything to do with the status of esteem (of my parents, not of me). My father moved to Westcliff-on-sea in 1912, to a newly formed Congregational church, Crowstone. I received a great deal of friendly regard from his large and warm-hearted congregation through the next fifteen years, and, of course, I was very much a part of the life of the church from my earliest years, though more, it would be true to say, from circumstances than conviction.

In the 1920's our house was suddenly full of architects' drawings – entries in a competition for the winning design for the new church. Only the big church hall had so far existed. I was delighted to get away from boarding school for the foundation stone laying in 1924, and again two years later for the opening of the magnificent new church, sometimes called in those days the cathedral of Congregationalism. Fifty years later I was privileged to take part in the service for its jubilee. It looked more beautiful than ever. In the 1960's I often thought of father in those distant years and how he battled not just for funds but even more for the quality and perfection of the building, when I was engaged in building operations which were also to the glory of God, at the Westminster Theatre.

Through all this time my father was becoming increasingly well known as a preacher and thinker in the Church, as a writer (I remember the publication of the first of his forty-two books in the early 1920's) and as an exponent of the social application and obligations of the Christian faith.

In 1924, father was invited for the second year running to take part in one of Sir Henry Lunn's ecumenical conferences at Mürren, in the Swiss Oberland. This time my mother and I went too. Here we mingled with men of distinction in the

Churches who were uniformly kind to me as a shy twelve-year old. Among them were James Moffat, whose translation of the Bible was a landmark, and Archbishop Nathan Soderblöm of Sweden, with his shock of white hair, who was a great pioneer of the ecumenical movement, and a most warm-hearted man. There were writers like Paul Sabatier, politicians like Isaac Foot, theologians like Dr. Deissmann and Adolf Keller, bishops, denominational leaders like Dr. Scott Lidgett, and many more. One man I did not meet but saw and heard lecture there was Arnold Lunn, Sir Henry's son, who forty years later became a warm friend of my wife and myself.

Although my father was the most charitable of men, full of goodwill and affection even for his most troublesome opponents, he was usually in hot water for something he had said or some stand he had taken. Yet he had an immensely devoted following at Crowstone and later at Whitefields Central Mission in London, where 1,500 people packed the huge old church in Tottenham Court Road every Sunday evening to hear him. (The church was destroyed by one of the last V2 rockets of the war. It has been rebuilt, on a more modest scale, and is now the American Church in London.)

Father had a brilliant and versatile mind, coupled with a bubbling sense of humour, and he pioneered in many fields, including the application of psychology to Christian counselling long before this became accepted practice. He gained a growing reputation on both sides of the Atlantic, and many of the senior political figures were his friends, from President Roosevelt to the leadership of the British Labour Party. It was a lasting experience for me to accompany him in 1927, aged fifteen, on the first of his many long preaching and lecturing tours in the United States and Canada. It left me with an abiding affection for the far side of the Atlantic. It was also the last time I crossed the Atlantic in a properly civilised manner, on the Berengaria and the Aquitania, with their superlative and enormous menus, ideally suited to my schoolboy appetite.

During the first twenty years of my life I was automatically a part of my father's churches and saw many issues through his eyes and insights, and through the innumerable books on his shelves, to which I always had unlimited access from my earliest years. Father's books were wide-ranging: the poets, the English classics and modern novels, psychology, social issues, religion of course and philosophy, biography, history and much more besides, including two sets of illustrated encyclopedias which I browsed in by the hour as a boy.

Through all this time, however, my faith, such as it was, was entirely second-hand. In one way I knew it all, because it had been a daily part of life for as long as I could remember. At a certain level I accepted it all, or perhaps took it all for granted would be more accurate. At school I would sometimes pray fervently at crisis moments with exams or the chance of getting into the 1st XV, but there was no way in which faith really impinged on my life. Religion and church-going bored me.

The reason was that I could find no relation between the faith I had been brought up in and the life I was actually living. All that I knew of faith seemed powerless in face of the realities of my own nature, in my own situation. Faith simply didn't work as far as I was concerned and, due to my own obtuseness no doubt, I felt that no one had ever suggested that it would in terms that I could grasp and apply practically.

Socialism, capitalism, re-armament, pacifism, class-war – these I could understand, but not how to find the grace of God in my life, the guidance of God to direct me, or the power of God to change me. No one had ever told me about the concrete problems they themselves had been delivered from, the miracles in themselves or other people that followed because God had said to them, "Do this" or "Speak to that man." It might have happened two or three millenia ago, but the idea of a God who could actually do anything in the twentieth century was remote from my expectations – anything useful, that is, anything practical, anything visible and effective in the places where it would mean something to people, anything which could transform a given person or situation.

To father, taking a lead in church or community, speaking, preaching, writing, all came naturally, or so it looked to me. He lived his life fearlessly and cheerfully in terms of his own faith and the burning issues of the world. I was more like my mother, who was a deeply fearful person behind the many courageous things she did. Fear was a considerable factor in my life, leading to a paralysing shyness: fear especially of what other people thought of me, fear of being caught in some situation I wouldn't know how to handle, fear of speaking in public (that was total), fear of taking any sort of lead except amongst my few closest cronies, fear of any new or unexpected developments in life . . . the list is a long one.

This was matched by a sense of having no real purpose. Nowadays people in their twenties seem to go around looking for their identity – who am I? It never crossed my mind to doubt my identity: what I wanted was an aim in life. Nothing remotely like a "call" to any particular work or place ever came my way. I hoped that one day I would find something to which I could give the whole of myself, something which would compel the allegiance of my whole being and magnetise my meagre powers, but as time went by I despaired of finding it. I knew my father's crowning desire was for me to go into the ministry, but that was the worst of all. Think of having to stand up and deliver two different sermons every Sunday of your life! Unthinkable.

At the same time, of course, all the fantasies and manifestations of sex were sweeping over me. They got going a little later than with some of my friends, but when they did I was carried away on the tide like anyone else.

In these three fields of fear, aim and conduct, the faith I had been brought up in seemed singularly impotent. God may have delivered the heroes of the Old and New Testaments from fear, but He wasn't delivering me. He may have spoken to the prophets or the early Christians in the Acts of the Apostles, but it never crossed my mind that He could speak to me, now. And as for delivering me from the power of overwhelming habits or traits or character, that was as improbable as anything else, if not more so.

By the time I reached Oxford in 1931 my faith, such as it was, had gone. At politest I was an agnostic. In practice I was an atheist, and like all atheists I was locked up, I thought for ever, in the prison cell of my own nature, my own heredity, my own manifest shortcomings. It looked like a life sentence.

But, had I known it, my situation was already a little like those days on the sea-shore when the sea seems miles away across the sands, and then suddenly you find the incoming tide swirling round your feet and pouring in fast, because you were unaware that it had turned. And had I had the wit to see it, that turn of the tide had begun in my last term at school.

2
You never know where lightning will strike

"The head wants us in his drawing room tonight," a friend called out to me in the corridor one Sunday, in my last months at school. "Us" was a group of senior boys who were sometimes convened by the Headmaster, A. P. Mottram, on Sunday evenings for an informal talk on some "serious" subject. I am afraid we often treated these occasions with more ribaldry than they deserved, since he meant well and was a kindly host.

This particular evening proved to be out of the ordinary run. The speaker was an Old Boy of the school, Bernard Chutter, a rotund and rollicking character who was, surprisingly, at an Oxford theological college. Even more unexpectedly, he had recently undergone an experience, he told us, which had radically altered his life for the better and freed him from pressing and persistent problems. He had been brought in touch with some interesting people called the Oxford Group whose views he strongly recommended for our consideration.

Looking back now I can see that he could have been a good deal more concrete in some of his explanations, but it was plain that something considerable had happened to the man and that, as he firmly emphasised, it was all based on a complete surrender of his life to God. Anyone could find the same experience in the same way: it was simply a question of giving everything to Christ.

All this became so clear in the course of the evening that the more I thought about it the more I was repelled by it. I felt dead against it. The whole idea was too upsetting to entertain for a moment. I was so certain that the deepest things in my life could never be changed, least of all by total surrender to a God I hardly believed in, that to act on the lines Bernard suggested would entail an upheaval which it was too painful to contemplate and which, I was convinced, was bound to prove fruitless. It could not work. I knew these things in my nature could not be shifted. Why stir it all up needlessly? It could only deepen my despair. It was the typical frustration of the atheist, trapped in his own character, and the only course open to me seemed to be wholehearted resistance.

So I began freely and frequently to criticise Bernard and his friends in the Oxford Group, and to make sage and authoritative-sounding remarks to all and sundry about the "psychological dangers" of what they proposed, and generally to steer very clear of them when I arrived in Oxford myself – and all this based on the meagre information gleaned on that one evening at school, plus a certain amount of common-room gossip at the University.

A strange thing happened early in my second year, however, which brought me up sharply and helped pave the way for what was to follow, though outwardly there seemed no connection. I had moved out of college into lodgings up the Iffley Road, conveniently opposite the University rugger ground, and a man I had been at school with was sharing the rooms with me. I didn't really know him very well, but finding ourselves both in need of lodgings we had teamed up together.

One day I was browsing through the old Davenant bookshop in the High when I took from the second-hand shelves a large volume – a dictionary of English history. I was surprised to see it, as I had seen very few copies around the University, and one of them was on my own shelves. I was even more surprised – dumbfounded indeed – on opening it to discover it was my own copy – with my name crossed out but still legible! I scouted round a bit and found some other books of mine. Someone had been stealing them and selling them, and when I talked to the book shop staff it was clear it could only be my roommate. That evening I taxed him with it, and he admitted he had done it because he was very short of money. So was I for that matter, being a parson's son – this was before the State paid for university education. He apologised emotionally and repaid the money for me to get the books back.

But I was deeply troubled. How could such a thing happen, and what could I do about it? What was my responsibility to a friend who could be pushed into doing something so unpleasant? I even went and talked it over with my Vice-Principal, John Brewis, who was tutoring me that term and was in Holy Orders. Did he think I ought to put my room-mate in touch with the Oxford Group? Evidently I thought they might do something for him even though I had no intention of letting them do anything for me. John Brewis wisely refused to let me get away with this. "It's not a question of whether other people could do something for him," he said. "The question is, what are you going to do for him? He's your friend and your responsibility."

This was perfectly true. But I hadn't the faintest idea what to do, and John Brewis didn't tell me, so I did nothing at all. My room-mate and I parted company not long after, and I lost touch with him for some years. Then, long after Oxford, I heard from him, from the West Indies. He was dying of tuberculosis, but although he knew he had very little time to live, he had found a living faith in Jesus Christ and wanted me to know. I wrote back at once, and had one further letter from him just before the end.

Although I felt I did nothing for him in those unhappy days at Oxford because I had nothing to give him, he gave a great deal to me, because the whole episode jerked me out of my preoccupation with myself and brought me hard up against the fact that I had nothing to offer a fellow human being who was in trouble.

A few weeks later, Christmas brought another unpredictable event. You never know where the lightning will strike next. When I arrived home at the end of term I found my mother, naturally enough, doing up parcels for friends and relations and getting out Christmas cards. Among the presents waiting to be wrapped up was a book with a striking cover in black and red. Its title: *For Sinners Only*, by

A. J. Russell, a Fleet Street editor. On enquiry I found to my surprise that my father intended it as a present for my Aunt Clarice (an action on his part which has never been explained, but presumably was due to one of those promptings of Providence which you think is aimed at one bird but actually brings down another. Since Clarice's death I have kept that copy, found among her books, on my own shelves.)

Anyway, it looked interesting and I took it off and read it. *For Sinners Only,* was one of the first and most compelling books about the Oxford Group. I was spellbound from the start. Some of the people in it I actually knew. One of them even lived in our road at home and his brother was a friend of mine in my own college. Many others were so like myself and my friends that I seemed to be treading familiar ground – and yet the whole book was like a window opened onto a new and absorbingly interesting territory.

It was evidently a world where things happened, where people were transformed, however deep-seated or impossible their troubles; a world of purpose because God, they said, has a plan for every human life and will speak to you and unfold it to you day by day if you give Him the chance; a world of inner freedom, inner certainty, where faith is effective, where you can break out of the prison cell of your own self-centredness, or rather where the door can be unlocked for you, and the wide world with its tumultuous needs and endless opportunities lies before you.

I was particularly struck by the fact, emphasised

many times in the book, that these people had found that when they took time to be quiet and listen, especially in the early morning, God would speak to them: He would put thoughts into their minds which would guide their lives and, even more important, enable them to help others who might be in need. I felt increasingly drawn to the people in the book and the experiences they recounted. They had the ring of reality about them.

Needless to say, I said nothing of all this to my family or to my friends up the road, but I went back to Oxford for the new term inwardly decided to find out more about it all.

Events moved faster than I expected. The evening I arrived back, I strolled into the rooms of a friend of mine in college to pass the time of day with him. He wasn't there, but standing on his hearthrug was a man who had gone down the year before and was now at Cuddesdon theological college.

"Hullo Jack," I said, "what are you doing here?"

Jack Torrens replied cheerfully, "I'm here on guidance."

Now you might think this a foolish reply to make to a beefy, pipe-smoking, pagan-hearted agnostic. But inwardly I was transfixed. "Here's one of them actually doing it", I thought to myself, remembering what I had so recently read in A. J. Russell's book. What I said to Jack was, "Oh, really?"

Undeterred by this non-committal reply, Jack put his hand into his pocket and brought out a large white card, impeccably printed by the Oxford University Press. "We're having a meeting next Sunday night at the Randolph Hotel," he said. "Some of our people are just back from a campaign across Canada. Perhaps you'd like to come."

I pocketed the card. "Well – I might," I replied, and left as fast as I could.

But inwardly I wanted to go and see for myself. I knew I was coming nearer to something that might be crucial for my life. The following Sunday I took a friend for protection and rolled up at the meeting. We sat in the back row in the Randolph ballroom, puffing our pipes. Half way through we strolled out, in the casual Oxford manner of those days. But I had heard enough to know that this was it as far as I was concerned. This was reality. Here was hope. And something deep in me responded.

The speakers, all brief and vivid, were a varied lot, introduced by Roland Wilson of Oriel, who was to be one of my closest friends and colleagues over many years. Some were undergraduates, some senior Oxford, including Kirstie Morrison, later Senior Tutor at St. Annes when my daughter Hilary was there, and Professor L. W. Grensted, one of Oxford's leading theologians and psychologists – only he wasn't talking about theology or psychology but about the change in his own life and the lessons he had learned travelling across Canada with an international team of sixty of the Oxford group. Another man who caught my attention was Ian Sciortino, from my own college. When he first came up the term before I had gloomily forecast from his excessively good-looking, devil-may-care manner, that he would undoubtedly go to the dogs in his first year.

But here he was, three months later, telling the University how Christ had transformed his life in the intervening period. I was considerably shaken.

The following week I invited the man I knew best in the Group to tea in my lodgings. This was Donal Browne, a large, lantern jawed, slow speaking, humorous eyed Irishman, a rock-like character. I asked him what meeting with the Oxford Group had meant to him, and he told me, quietly, methodically, without fanfare. As time went on I panicked inwardly. What if this man asks me to make a decision for my life? I was terrified of this, not simply because it would be launching into the unknown but more because I felt that if I ever made such a decision I wanted it to be entirely of my own volition, so that I could never say later, if the going got rough, "Well, I was pushed into it so I needn't stick to it."

I need not have worried. When Don got to the end of what he had to say he just got up and said, "Well, I must go now. I have to meet some people. Thanks for the tea. Goodbye."

Next day I ran into Don in the front quad. "Oh, by the way," he said, "we're having a meeting here in college on Sunday evening, as a follow-up to that Randolph meeting. I thought you might like to come."

"Well, I might," I said, and left it at that.

Turning it over in my mind, I thought that if I went to this meeting I had better go somewhat better equipped. I knew a man who happened to have a copy of *For Sinners Only*, so I borrowed it from him. Next Sunday, the day of the meeting, I read it again from cover to cover and began to feel more deeply than ever that this pointed in the direction I should be going. But could I? Had I the nerve?

Before setting out for the meeting I thought to myself, "Why don't you try one of these quiet times they talk about and see whether God, if there is a God, says anything to you? You can do it here by yourself, and no one need ever know."

I cannot remember the half-dozen thoughts which went through my mind as I sat there quietly and duly wrote them down, as the people did in the book. But right at the end one thought came into my mind with crystal clarity, and I also wrote it down: "You will give your life to Me tonight."

With this unnerving forecast in my pocket I headed into college. Don was waiting for me in the quad. "Which would you rather do," he asked me, "would you like to go to this meeting or shall we go and have a talk together somewhere?"

"Oh," I said, "I'd much rather talk with you." Don, as his large London parishes later discovered, was already a wise man of God in dealing with people. No meeting that evening could have done for me what the talk with Don accomplished.

We talked away for an hour in Ian Sciortino's rooms as he was out at the meeting. Then at one point I said, "I can see the places where I most need to change in my life," (and indeed they were only too painfully plain to me) "but I can't for the life of me see how they can change. I've tried often enough."

Don replied and turned my world upside down.

He said simply, "God can do for you the things you can't do for yourself." I had never heard such a statement before. It was the first glint of hope. "All you have to do," he said, "is give your life to Him."

Then he said, "Shall we have a quiet time together and see what thoughts God has for us?"

I was in a dilemma. I could hardly say "No", or "What do you mean?" as I had been trying out a quiet time myself a couple of hours before. But if I said "Yes", where would it lead to? All my fears rose up, and yet another part of me wanted to take the risk and go forward. So I agreed, but I did not let on that I knew people in the Group wrote their thoughts down. So Don wrote his in a little notebook and I did not. It made no difference to the outcome.

After a time he asked me, "What came to you?" I told him. For the first time in my life I told someone else about the deepest things that troubled me. It was the measure of my confidence in him as a friend as well as an inner movement of the grace I still knew nothing about. I cannot remember what Don's thoughts were, but a little later he clearly felt the moment for something more decisive had arrived, and said quite gently, "Wouldn't you like to give your life to God now?"

"No thanks!" I exclaimed, jumping to my feet and heading for the door. "I must go now. Goodnight."

So I fled out of college, down the High, across Magdalen bridge, along the Iffley Road to my lodgings, up the stairs to my bedroom, and there I got down on my knees – and gave my life to God. It was still on the level of "God – if there is a God – I give you my life." But I meant it, and I knew I had taken the most momentous step of my life.

Next morning I got up half an hour earlier, which was a revolution in itself, and sat in my dressing gown beside the gas fire in my bedroom, on a freezing January morning, for my first morning quiet time.

I was somewhat at a loss what do to. So I picked up a devotional book which my father had once given me and which, needless to say, I had never opened. I opened it now, on these verses from Psalm 143 which I had never seen before: "Hear my prayer, O Lord, give ear to my supplications; in Thy faithfulness answer me and in Thy righteousness. Cause me to hear Thy loving kindness in the morning, for in Thee do I trust; cause me to know the way wherein I should walk, for I lift up my soul unto Thee. Teach me to do Thy will, for Thou art my God; Thy spirit is good: lead me in the land of uprightness."

It could not have been tuned more accurately to my need, and I was deeply stirred by it. Then I thought perhaps I should read something from the New Testament, of which I was extraordinarily ignorant considering the amount of it I had listened to in my life. But I remembered there was something called the Sermon on the Mount, and ran it to earth with the help of the headlines in my Bible (a leaving gift from school which had long gathered dust in my bedroom.) The verses which spoke to me with sudden clarity were, "Ask, and it shall be given you; seek and you shall find; knock and it shall be opened unto you", promises which re-assured me greatly.

As I read these passages and sat there quietly turning them over in my mind, I knew beyond all doubt that a change of earthquake proportions had taken place deep inside me since the night before and that life would never be the same again. I felt I was free at last from the things that had dogged me for so long. And in the silence, even at that early stage, I began to be aware that Jesus Christ Himself had come into my consciousness as a living reality, with the power to make everything different, in a way I had never known or dreamed of before, and with a peace in my heart which was entirely new to me.

It was only later that I came to know these lines of Richard Crashaw:

> When love of us called Him to see
> If we'd vouchsafe His company,
> He left His Father's court and came
> Lightly as a lambent flame
> Leaping upon the hills, to be
> The humble King of you and me.
> Nor can the cares of His whole crown
> (When one poor sigh sends for Him down)
> Detain Him, but He leaves behind
> The late wings of the lazy wind,
> Spurns the tame laws of time and place
> And breaks through all ten heavens to our
>   embrace.
> Yield to His siege, wise soul, and see
> Your triumph in His victory.
> Disband dull fears, give faith the day,
> To save your life, kill your delay. . . .

> Yield then, O yield, that love may win
> The fort at last, and let life in.

My start may have been shaky the night before, but now life was indeed pouring in. As I sat there, I wrote down my thoughts: to write my parents a full and honest letter; to repay money that I owed – simple steps of this sort to clear the decks. Then came the thought to go and call on a friend of mine after breakfast.

This was an unexpected idea. He was one of my best friends from school, and was at another college. I would never dream of calling him at nine in the morning when he was probably rushing to a tutorial or a lecture or wildly finishing an essay. But I had the thought, so I went. I found him ill in bed and needing medical care, which I was able to set in motion for him. A small event, but the first time I had done anything for someone else because God sent me, and the first time I realised that God might know more about even a familiar situation than I knew myself.

Above all, that first morning's quiet time filled me with a sense of the presence of the living God surrounding me, and the knowledge that the prison doors of my own self had opened onto sunlit horizons of limitless promise.

After seeing my friend, I thought I had better go and find Don who I had abandoned so unceremoniously the night before, and tell him what had happened. I ran into him in college and told him my tale, which he took with his usual imperturbability. He thought for a bit. Then he said, "Well, that means you're on the team now."

"What's that?" I enquired. It was a new idea to me.

"Oh," he said, "it's all of us who try to live by God's guidance in the University. We meet at one-thirty every day in the Old Library at St. Mary's (the University Church). You'd better come along today."

"What do you do there?" I asked him.

"Well," he said, "we share our experiences of what it means to live the Christian life, and we study the Bible together and we get training in how to win people and how we can be more effective." Then he added casually, "We always give the news of what's been happening in our different colleges since the day before. Of course, today you're our news, so you'd better give it."

My world collapsed about me. Me? Speak to eighty or a hundred people I had never seen before about my practically non-existent Christian experience of a few hours? I was appalled. I couldn't do it. I was finished before I had begun. All the fears of all the years met in me at that moment.

I said nothing, but crawled away to think about it in the rooms of a friend who was thankfully out at the time.

"Well," I thought, "you'd better try one of these quiet times. It looks as though you need it." So I did. And I wrote down the one thought that came to me: "If God wants you to do something He will give you the strength to do it."

So I went along to the Old Library with Don, and it was packed with men and women I had never set eyes on before. The meeting was being led by Madeleine Allen, wife of Geoffrey Allen, then chaplain of Jesus College. The atmosphere was informal and friendly, and at the appropriate moment I rose and told my tale (at inordinate length I imagine, looking back). But for the first time in my life I felt completely at ease speaking to a large group of people, and this in itself was a major miracle for me.

Indeed, I think Don and the others must have realised this, because first I was asked, after the meeting, if I would join a group at tea where we were to speak to interested friends, and then I was invited to join a similar occasion in a friend's rooms in my own college after supper. Soon after I arrived at this event I found myself surrounded by an incredulous group of old cronies whose main aim seemed to be to dislodge me from my precarious hold on my new-found faith. They obviously felt it was a lamentable lapse which I urgently needed to snap out of. All I could say to most of their unhelpful interrogations was, "Well, I know nothing about that. All I know is that something has happened to me since I gave my life to God last night, and I know I'm different deep down inside and free from the things that troubled me."

Some people are keener to get you out of the Christian faith than to get you in. Especially if you have found it through people of whom they disapprove or in a way that makes them feel uncomfortable.

It was a gruelling evening, and I don't know how much it did for the others, but it certainly did a lot for me: from that time onwards I have never again feared to speak to an audience. It was a tough but liberating series of events that first day which all showed that Christ could give me freedom at the very places in my life where I thought change was most impossible. If He could do that for me He could do anything for anyone.

The other unexpected outcome of the day was my new-found friends. I was launched on the most extraordinary adventure – in company with a group of friends I had met during that day, and many more in the following days, most of whom are still alive and working together more than half a century later.

3
"I call you friends"

> He wakes desires you never may forget,
> He shows you stars you never saw before,
> He makes you share with Him for evermore
> The burden of the world's Divine regret.
> How wise you were to open not – and yet
> How poor if you should turn Him from the door.

I do not know who Sydney Lysaght was who wrote these lines, and I found them on a calendar more than fifty years ago. But they capture something of the strangeness and the marvel of the existence I had now stepped into.

It is a bit unnerving for the average atheist or agnostic to move, from one day to the next, into a world where the God he had not believed in is discovered to be a living Person with the power to change the most intractable elements of his own make up, with the implication that this same unseen but effective Force is available for anyone; to find the prison cell of his old self gone, to know that he is free – and no longer alone.

Hard on this comes the discovery that this hitherto unknown God speaks to men, to you yourself: that as soon as any man or woman makes space and time, and willingness, in their hitherto overcrowded and empty lives, He is there to direct and encourage and lead out into the lives of other people. You suddenly become aware that a world of hitherto unknown needs surrounds you, but you now know where those needs can be met. The indwelling Spirit is becoming a reality.

But even more, beyond losing the profound isolation of the agnostic, that chilling belief that I am alone in an impersonal universe, is the discovery of a transforming friendship. It is the growing awareness that Christ is not only "the Captain of our salvation", forgiving us and freeing us from the sins of the years, He is not only the incarnation of the limitless love of God for all men everywhere, "the visible expression of the invisible God", as St. Paul calls him: He is also our companion of the road, our friend in every need, at hand in every sorrow, in every rejoicing; the pioneer of our battle for a remade world. He said, "I call you friends".

It is hard to put all this into words. The full realisation of the meaning of these mighty experiences can take a lifetime to explore and understand. Yet they were all there in that first twenty-four hours in January 1933, and in the immediate days and weeks that followed. I remember once flying over the Rockies from the Alberta prairies deep in snow and sub-zero temperatures, and landing an hour or two later in Vancouver in spring sunshine and a blaze of flowers. It was like that, from winter into springtime.

There was one aspect of this new existence that was in some ways almost as surprising to me, as I mentioned earlier: the discovery of my friends.

"God setteth the solitary in families", says the

Psalmist, and this is exactly what happened. I had always been solitary, by nature and by preference, the proverbial only child. So I missed a lot of some aspects of family life, and was not too sorry to have done so. But such a life has its drawbacks, and the effect of course was to make me far too inturned and excessively self-centred.

All that was turned around 180 degrees by my encounter with that team in Oxford. Not that self-centredness is eliminated in a day or a lifetime, but the process had begun with dramatic suddenness.

I soon began to put names to the rows of unknown faces at the daily meetings in the Old Library at St. Mary's. Indeed, one of the endearing things about them was the way person after person came to make himself known to me, and how many of them, one by one, took the time, often on long afternoon walks along the towpath by the river, to share with me the story of their own lives and what Christ had done for them, and listen to mine, so that people I had never met before became friends for life at a level of mutual understanding and knowledge unknown to me before, even in the best of my earlier friendships. They had in them the honesty and self-knowledge of committed men.

The next thing I realised was that this was no mutual admiration society: it was not just fellowship for the pleasure of it. This was the comradeship of an army in battle. There was salt in it, not sugar. I discovered rapidly that these men and women were engaged in a daily, self-sacrificing hand to hand effort to win their contemporaries to the vital experience of Christ which they themselves had found, and that they went to infinite trouble to bring this about.

I had no idea such things were going on in the University. Even in my own college I found we were a team of half-a-dozen or more, and we met daily. To my amazement I found that between them they knew where virtually every man in the place stood in relation to the claims of Christ on his life. They prayed for them, they sought to understand their needs and how best to help, or win their interest, or overcome their scepticism and looked for natural openings to talk with them, not ham-handedly (usually) but sensitively and, to the best of their ability, as God led them. They did not impose themselves, as they had never imposed themselves on me, but they tried to build the kind of friendships where the other man could, if he wished, have enough confidence to talk about the deepest things on his mind, as I had done with Don.

This was indeed a new kind of existence, with aims utterly different from leading a solitary, inturned life doing only the things that pleased or interested me. Every other concern was subordinated to reaching the needs of people and learning the skills to do so, and there are plenty of needs in a university, as the high rate of student suicide shows. It was a training ground in some of the basic aspects of our calling. "Follow Me, and I will make you fishers of men".

It was at times a life of constant miracles of change in all kinds of people. At others, try as we might, nothing much seemed to happen, and we settled down to working away without much to show for it. Then at a touch from the Spirit, it seemed, person after person would step into our ranks, with consequences that are still being felt in many lands around the world.

One day, a few weeks after I began, I was having a snack lunch by myself in my lodgings, in the midst of an essay for my tutor, when the thought dropped lightly as a falling feather into my mind that what I had experienced in the previous weeks pointed to my life's calling. For me it was not to be the settled professional life I was preparing for, but to take the road wherever it led, to live by faith and prayer without salary or security if need be, to move out with my friends to do what we could to tackle the world as God showed us.

I knew that the vast majority of people in the Oxford Group were active in their various jobs and occupations, but that a few were called to give their whole time, and it looked as if I were meant to be one of these.

There was nothing particularly insistent in the thought, just an intrinsic rightness which I accepted, though I had no idea how or where it was to be carried out. The thought persisted through my last two years at the University, and when I finally took my degree and went down, I felt ready and full of anticipation for the uncertain future that lay ahead.

I hadn't the least idea how I would live. I often reread hopefully the passage in St. Matthew which says, "Seek ye first the Kingdom of God and His righteousness, and all these things shall be added unto you", but how could this work out in practice? And could such a promise possibly hold true at a time when there were three million unemployed, and I could think of no obvious resources that might be available for me? I knew that there were no central funds in the Oxford Group and no salaries, and that every whole-time worker was expected to live by his own faith, and to help his friends where he could. It felt a bit like jumping out of a plane without a parachute. But in my bones I knew it was my calling.

It was not until six months later that I met Frank Buchman, the extraordinary genius behind the worldwide expansion of the Oxford Group. I met him that summer at the first Oxford House Party, as they were called, which I had been to. Summer by summer, over an eight week period, several thousand people passed through these House Parties – centred on four colleges as a rule, with united meetings for everyone at weekends in the Town Hall or in St. Mary's, the University Church. By 1933 the Oxford Group was already active in fifty countries, so there were people from all round the globe on these occasions.

It was illuminating to see Buchman in action. Although he sometimes led stimulating meetings his main aim seemed to be to encourage others to take a lead. He was never the lone-star performer. "Better set ten men to work than do ten men's work", he often said.

Around Frank there always seemed to be the crackle of miracles and the unpredictability of the

Spirit's promptings, along with the exhilarating vision of new horizons for our lives. His aim was always to find God's direction, in matters great and small. He was leading one of the evening meetings at that first House Party, in Lady Margaret Hall, one of the four centres. To my surprise he suddenly whispered to one of the others on the platform to take over the meeting, got up and left the room. A quarter of an hour later he returned, and explained, "I had guidance to leave the meeting. Outside I found someone who had been suddenly taken ill, with no one to help, and I was able to find a doctor and see she was properly cared for."

There was always a touch of the unexpected with him, mixed with a good deal of hilarity among the varied group of people I found moving with him, some very able and many very ordinary, but all caught with the possibilities the Holy Spirit held out for reaching ever widening circles of people, and salted with equally unexpected depths of insight into the spiritual needs of people, ourselves included. "You've got to learn to read people like a page of print."

I also discovered how generous he was in his care for everyone, young or old, veteran or newly arrived, as I was. After the Christmas term that same year, a House Party was held at Eastbourne to which many of us went down from Oxford. One of those present was the Hon. Carl Hambro, President of the Norwegian Parliament, and President of the League of Nations. He had met Buchman some months before, in Geneva and rated what he heard from him as "more important that most of the agenda of the League that year." During the House Party Buchman was invited to bring a group up to Westminster, to address Members of Parliament – who crowded the Grand Committee Room in the House of Commons. I had been asked to drive some people up in a car someone had lent, so there I was, aged twenty-one, at the wheel of a 3½ litre Bentley, thoroughly enjoying myself. (The first and last time I ever drove a Bentley.)

At the House of Commons, I was asked if I would drive Hambro back to Eastbourne after the meeting. When Frank heard of this, he said to me, "You must join us at dinner first." "Dinner" was specially given for him and a few senior men in the House of Lords dining room, by Lord Rochester, the Paymaster General. The guests present were Hambro, the Hon. Carl Vrooman, who had been under-Secretary for Agriculture in President Wilson's administration in Washington, Dr. Jan de Bordes, Finance Secretary to the League of Nations in Geneva, Loudon Hamilton and John Roots, two of Frank's closest co-workers, Frank himself – and me. Buchman was silent, deep in his own thoughts, for much of the meal, and I, for obvious reasons, said nothing at all. But the others! I have never heard before or since such a torrent of hilarious stories. Loudon Hamilton, of course, was a master of Scottish tales, and Carl Vrooman of dry American humour. John Roots, a fellow American, and de Bordes chimed in occasionally. But the star of the evening was Hambro himself, whose command of English humour was superbly accurate, and kept the party in fits of laughter. It was an eye-opener to me on how statesmen behave when they are off duty! It was typical of Buchman to have invited me when I was just the driver, and a youngster at that. He loved including people like this, for their enjoyment and also their education.

I realised as time went on that Frank was always planning imaginative strokes that would win people and make an impact on whole communities and even countries, and that often these hinged on particular people in those countries. At that House of Commons meeting, Hambro, in addressing the MPs, had invited Frank Buchman to bring the Oxford Group to Norway. The following winter, he went with a team of twenty-five. Hambro invited 120 people to meet them at a hotel outside Oslo – and 1,200 turned up. It was the beginning of a movement of the Spirit that was felt up and down the land and still continues. A leading Oslo daily wrote, "A handful of foreigners who neither knew our language or understood our ways and customs came to this country . . . A few days later the whole country was talking about God, and two months after they arrived, the mental outlook of the country had definitely changed."

Life around Buchman had its moments when the lightning crackled about our heads, if something had gone wrong or been done inadequately. But he never held our shortcomings against us. It gave us all a sense of battle, and training in what was needed to bring help to a disordered world.

What caught my imagination were his strenuous attempts to lift our minds to the scale on which God wanted His followers to act – "the full scope of the majesty of what needs to be done." With this went his unending search for fresh ways of expressing and presenting truth in order to reach people in an increasingly Godless world, together with new reaches of experience in people's lives which would win a modern generation. "You can always take people as far as you have gone yourself."

He insisted we must be bi-lingual, and speak the language of the ordinary man as well as of Christian piety. To one wayward and brilliant student at Oxford, whose main preoccupation, in a notorious motor cycle club, was fast bikes and fast girls, he said, "You know how to mend bikes. Come with us and learn how to mend people." It captured the young man's attention. It led him by stages to a full commitment to Christ. He then took a First Class degree in theology and entered on a lifetime of service.

Frank's constant preoccupation was how to set people on fire and give their lives to "the greatest revolution of all time, whereby the Cross of Christ will transform the world." All this he pursued with passion, laughter, originality and courage, and a belief in what any and every person could do, once their life was committed wholly to God. And in this his greatest weapon, as I soon discovered, was the team.

4
Secret of teamwork

IN THE Oxford Group, as I found in those first months, we believed in moving with a team wherever we could. Frank Buchman could so easily have been the star turn in any campaign. Instead he spent his life building teams of people and training them, so that they could carry their message further than any individual could by himself. The variety of a team meant that no one could say "they're not my kind of people." And, as Norway clearly demonstrated, the effect of a team on a country could be electrifying.

Following Norway, there came pressing appeals from people in Denmark. Buchman felt that the only way to make headway in that charming but cynical country was to take a large enough team to make an immediate public impact. "We must go to the court of public opinion", he said. He took a team of 300. I was invited to be one of them. We were all ages, nationalities and backgrounds.

We started with a week of meetings every night in a hall in the middle of Copenhagen, rather like the old Queen's Hall in London. It held perhaps a thousand people. Night by night it was packed, with speakers of all ages and backgrounds from our world-wide team. The first Dane to speak was our interpreter, who had been captivated and deeply changed that week. During and after this week we fanned out all over the city and to other parts of Denmark, as invitations came pouring in. The Press naturally gave it prominence and it was the talk of the country. One young man who had made a start was heard to say, "I am Oxford, three days". There was a considerable wave of being "Oxford" through the country, including industrial workers in the capital. One leading woman journalist wrote that she had come to interview Buchman, but it was he who had interviewed her – and she became a part of the Oxford Group ever afterwards.

At Easter, some weeks later, we gathered many hundreds of those who had responded for a long weekend in Haslev, a small town south of Copenhagen. It was full of boarding schools, empty over Easter, the only place with enough beds to get us all in.

One problem, as some of us knew from the past, was how to allocate people to their beds swiftly and accurately enough at such a conference. A friend and I invented a new "allocation board" in which every bed had a slot into which cards could go showing if it was free or who was in it. We had some samples made up by an old carpenter in a back street of Copenhagen. It worked like a charm under great pressure as so many arrived in a very short time, and we even had to allocate a Sheriff from Scotland to a bed in the town jail. The same allocation system is still in use in the Caux conference centre half a century later.

There followed further intensive activity in homes,

factories, churches, schools and elsewhere, and at Whitsun we gathered the whole three months together for a demonstration in Hamlet's castle at Elsinore, where the mighty quadrangle, like an Oxford or Cambridge college ten times the size, was packed with 10,000 people from all over Denmark and Scandinavia and further afield, including 300 from Holland who came by boat. It was a stirring sight from where I watched it, high in one of the corner towers. The main speakers were Danes, and Frank Buchman's short address was widely broadcast on radio.

A leading journalist, Carl Henrik Clemmensen, wrote afterwards in *Dagens Nyheder*: "Here was the whole castle courtyard packed as it had never been by any meeting hitherto. All ages were represented here, every party, every class, every stratum of society . . . Think of the remarkable things that happened: the distinguished actor-manager who stepped up to the platform and in his clear ringing voice read the story of the first Whit Sunday; the butcher from Nyborg, and the saddle-maker from Copenhagen, who stood side by side with the young Count and the Dean and witnessed to the new life they had found; a young concert singer from Finland in her beautiful national dress . . . the Bishop of Copenhagen . . . Professor Runestam, son-in-law of Archbishop Nathan Soderblöm, who on his very deathbed gave his blessing to the Oxford Group. And last of all came the Dean of Copenhagen, burning with zeal to proclaim in as personally stimulating and challenging a way as possible the message of the spiritual revolution which this means to the whole Danish people . . ."

The object of such occasions was to speak to the world, to whole countries and to individuals about the power of the living God and the scale on which He worked to move people and countries Godwards.

A year later I was back in Denmark. At Easter, the Danes arranged a long weekend in a vast covered stadium at Ollerup, in the centre island of Fyn (Hans Christian Andersen's home area.) The stadium held 15,000 and was filled through every day as people poured in by train, car, and, being Danes, by bicycle. These events spoke to the world through press and radio, and now film: we made our first short documentary film, *Bridgebuilders* in Denmark.

Once again, many of us stayed in schools. I shared a room with the headmaster of a British public school, a retired Indian Army general and a former communist worker from Slough. One cherished memory is the morning the ex-communist asked us all, "Has the general made the beds yet?" We took it in turns.

The following year we met at Whitsun on an even larger scale in the Netherlands, using the enormous Vegetable Market in Utrecht, the only building large enough to hold us all. My friend Peter Phelps and I took sixty people there from the South of England, where we worked at the time. Many stayed in Dutch homes, with generous hospitality. When we wanted to indicate that a meeting was about to take place, a team of twenty or thirty Scots would go round the town with bagpipes and drums, and the Dutch found the sound of the "doodlesacks" irresistible. Again, the message of God's redeeming power for men and women and their countries went out far beyond the Netherlands and echoed round the world. This was 1937, and war was only two years away.

Professor B. H. Streeter, the great New Testament scholar who was Provost of the Queen's college at Oxford, came up to me one day back in England and said, "Have you noticed how Frank Buchman has been led to move in such strength into the countries bordering on Germany?" It was a prescient comment. It was men and women from these countries, which suffered so much at the hands of Germany during the war, who moved into Germany afterwards with a message of hope and change as the road to a democratic future for that country.

We learned many things working in a team together. One thing I came to realise while we were in Denmark earlier was that one of the necessities of teamwork is independence: not the independence of self-assertiveness and self-will, but of being sure of God and depending on Him alone rather than on the approval or opinions of other people. As time went on during those months, I found myself beset by feelings of inadequacy. It was really, I think, a camouflaged desire for success. If only I were like so-and-so or so-and-so, men of stature and assurance who knew where they were going and gave a quiet but inspired lead to other people!

One day in some despondency I prayed about this and pondered it. We were having a few quiet days down by the sea, south of Copenhagen, during a short break in our campaign. As I listened, two thoughts came to me which changed my entire outlook permanently. The first was, "I don't want you to be a second somebody else: I want you to be the first yourself under the guidance of God." The second was, "Your life needs to hang by a string from God. If you hang by a string you can't lean on anything or anyone, and you don't need to." So I was freed to move in equal teamwork with my friends, and to forget about myself.

I often think that one of the most remarkable statements in the New Testament comes in the first letter of St. John: "We know that we have passed from death unto life because we love the brethren."

The more you think about it the more breathtaking it is. "We know" – this is the certainty of intuition – that because we love the people we work with for our faith we have already entered eternal life.

I cannot say that I have always managed to live like this. There have been times when I have born resentment against a colleague for something, real or imaginary (it makes no difference) which he has said or done that hurt me. Sometimes I have clung to it for years, even when we have been working together. And I have always found the answer has to start with me. I have to be prepared to change first, however much I feel the other person is to blame. I need to claim deliverance from my bitterness and apologise deeply and genuinely for it, and be simply honest about what started it. Often the other person is completely unaware of what has happened, and never intended what I thought. And of course the same sort of thing applies in married life as well.

One simple axiom is that bitterness is never right, and that God can always cure it, whether it is great or trivial. A few years ago, at a meeting of the Parochial Church Council in the village where we live, we were discussing the modern services we had been using in our church for some time. I made some point about the value of the language and atmosphere of the Prayer Book, to which a somewhat rough-tongued business man who was devoted to the modern forms called out "Rubbish!" – rather an unusual comment in the PCC. I was furious and thought, gloweringly, "Who does this fellow think he is? What does he know about it anyway?" Every time I thought of it in the next two or three weeks my hackles rose and I thought of smart things to say to put him in his place.

Then one morning in my quiet time came the thought, "You ought to love the man."

"Love him?" I thought. "Steady on Lord, that's asking too much. Maybe I can pray to swallow it all politely, but love him? How could I?"

"Well," came the reply, "You're both serving the church together. You'd better pray for love for him."

So I did, and the extraordinary thing was that I suddenly saw him in an entirely different light. I began to see what excellent qualities he had, how much he did in the life of the church, what a likeable man he really was; and perhaps my word in the PCC hadn't been all that perceptive in the circumstances, and anyway, he was entitled to his own opinion, even if he put it a bit strongly. So my wife and I invited him and his wife in for a meal, and then they asked us back. None of this was mentioned at the time, but I had changed inwardly, and we have been friends ever since.

Anna Letitia Waring puts it movingly:

> Wherever in the world I am,
> In whatso'er estate,
> I have a fellowship of hearts
> To keep and cultivate. . . .

A team is a prism through which the light streams in all its colours. But there is more to teamwork than gathering a group together for a particular occasion or to meet a local need. Teamwork calls for a deep level of understanding and knowledge of ourselves and of each other. It takes time and honesty, above all honesty about ourselves, a readiness to share our lives with each other in the deepest and most costly ways. Teamwork is not a method, and it is certainly not an optional extra. It is at the centre of our calling and of our effectiveness.

One key to community that I have found is my own need to become aware of the effect I may have on other people, which may be quite different from what I think it is, or think I intend. Once in the early part of the war, before I was called up, we were in the midst of a massive operation which called for a considerable volume of top-copy typing of a high order of accuracy (this was before the days of photocopiers or word processors.) I was in charge of this,

SECRET OF TEAMWORK

and imagined myself to be going out of my way to be considerate to the typists, all volunteers, who were carrying it out with devoted industry. But a candid colleague came to me and said, "The secretaries all feel you are driving them." I was mortified: it was the exact opposite of what I thought I was doing. As I pondered it, I realised that in me was an unspoken, indeed unrecognised, thrust of ambition: I wanted to show how well I could handle such an assignment, and this is what came across to the long-suffering secretaries, not my superficial good intentions.

Living in teamwork is in some ways like being married: you can no longer do just what suits you – not if you want it to last, anyway. You have to take someone else into account in everything you do, every decision, every move. It is your relationship, your evident unity which will speak to other people and win them, never your individualism. This sifts us down to our deepest thoughts and motives. Teamwork is like the tide washing over the pebbles on the beach: however hard they are, the sharp corners rub off in the end and a rounded product emerges!

As Frank Buchman often said, "It takes unselfishness to build a team." But it is the team which is so often God's instrument in the long run. What did the Founder of our faith leave as His plan for the world's redemption? A team of eleven apostles, 120 men and women gathered in an upper room, a group of friends "with one accord in one place."

5
The hour of the helicopter

> The Holy Spirit is the most intelligent source of information in the world today.
> Everywhere when men will let Him, He is teaching them how to live.
>
> *Frank Buchman*

IT WAS dawn in a remote village in the Papua-New Guinea Highlands in the early 1930's. A reveillé blown on conch shells summoned the villagers to gather with the chief and elders of the tribe. They met in silence, half an hour of silence together. Then they pooled the thoughts which the Spirit of God had given them.

Not long before, this was a head-hunting tribe, dominated by their witch doctors and the quest of murder. On this day, as they do week by week now, they are listening together to the living God. And He is altering the whole pattern of their lives. Head-hunting is out. They have made peace, over splendid feasts, with neighbouring tribes. Polygamy is going fast, by their own conviction. God's Spirit is re-shaping their whole mode of life, and soon will lead some of them out of their traditional mountain fastness to a new home on the plains, where they can start a rewarding programme of settled agriculture to replace the old ways of violent killing, and give a better standard of life to everyone. Nobody, black or white, is telling them what to do, but as they listen to the voice of God together and pursue the thoughts He gives them, they are finding step by step the way to go, not only as individuals but as a tribe. It is a social revolution, not imposed from outside but rising from within, and attuned to their natural needs as they are prepared to accept changes which would once have seemed unthinkable.

It was on a summer morning in London in 1935 that I first heard of this, in the sitting room in Browns Hotel which was part of our headquarters at the time. I heard it from Cecil Abel, of the pioneer missionary family in New Guinea. He had met the Oxford group some years before at Cambridge, and was responsible for initiating the hazardous expeditions into the Highlands, in places where no white man had been seen before, with a small group of friends, white and Papuan, who risked their lives to bring God's truth to some of the head-hunting tribes. He was on his way from Kwato in Papua to Oxford, for that year's Oxford House Party.

I was captivated. Here was a new dimension to what listening to God might lead to. He told me about a young man in the village who confronted the much feared witch doctor, who was known to kill people by his spells. With great courage he told him, "I will sleep over there on my veranda tonight and you can try any spell you like on me. Then we shall know whether your magic or my God is stronger." The witch doctor replied, "There's no point in doing that – I tried it last night. Your God is stronger than my magic." He was the next in the village to change. Forty years later the young man, Merari, by then in his sixties, came to see me when my wife and I were passing through Port Moresby. He was still going strong in the faith and playing his part in the newly independent Papua-New Guinea.

Nothing else I have experienced through the past fifty years has meant more to me than learning that quiet availability to the living God, especially in the early morning, when God Himself can speak to my mind and will, and when I can take Him into my life afresh. It is an hour when He lifts us to new levels of living and understanding – and action.

It is a tribute to the spiritual insight of Frank Buchman that he took an experience known to the Hebrew prophets and to Christians in the Acts of the Apostles and to so many others through the centuries, and showed that it can be available for everyone everywhere as a daily reality. To him it was the normal outcome of a committed life. There was nothing vague about it. Anyone whose life is unreservedly at God's disposal will be shown hour by hour, day by day, what He wants them to do, to be, if they will take the time to find out. As they obey, His plan unfolds.

This experience has become the daily bread of countless people the world over, from the common rooms of Oxford to the villages of Burma, from political leaders in Japan or Australia to miners in the Ruhr, farmers on the Canadian prairies, shipyard workers on the Clyde, diplomats at the United Nations or dockers in Rio and New York. These are all men and women who have based their lives not so much on occasional flashes of inspiration as on the daily, obedient waiting upon God which has enabled them to discern and fulfil His will for their lives.

How people spend their morning quiet time has many variations. I often start with reading a passage in the Old or New Testaments, or at other times from a book that feeds my spirit. Nearly every year I re-read William Temple's "Readings in St. John's Gospel", the gospel I most love. Each of us will find what is most nourishing for us. Then there are people to pray for – family, friends, particular needs of people we know, and so on. Often a thought comes which prompts us to pray for someone specially, for reasons we may discover afterwards.

But most of the time I spend quietly before God, putting myself at His disposal, writing down the thoughts that come to me. They may be few or many. Most may seem quite ordinary thoughts as I ponder the day ahead. Most of us are ordinary people leading ordinary lives. But as we think about what lies ahead in the coming day or days, the convictions grow in our minds about what we are meant to do, or say, in this situation or that. And as we listen, we are given the peace of heart and the confidence we need to go forward. We clearly feel one course is right, and another doubtful or even wrong. The name of someone often comes to us who we should see, or write to. Other thoughts may shed fresh light on the work we are doing, and the people we work with. Now and then unexpected insight comes into someone's difficulties, and what we could do to help.

My wife, too, would never miss that morning hour when God can give her the thoughts He wants her to have. Every now and then He illumines a question in her mind, or some need in someone else. She has a world-wide range of friends to think for and keeps up a constant correspondence with them. She also thinks daily for friends nearer home, and for our family – Hilary, Deputy Head of a large comprehensive school, David, Debi and our grandson Rowan in San Francisco. She also shows her care for people in her thought for the running of the home, something we do more together now than was possible in earlier years, and for the right meals for ourselves and when we entertain our friends.

So many sincere Christians believe that God can guide them, and I am sure He often does. But for many people their effectiveness could be multiplied many times over by giving God long enough every day.

Whatever may be the best time for night-duty nurses or night-shift workers, for the rest of us by far the best time for our quiet time is in the morning, before the rush of the day begins. After all, we map a journey before it begins, not afterwards. We can listen to God at any hour of the day or night, but the discipline and the courtesy of giving to God that first hour of the day makes a fundamental difference to life. What the real issue often turns out to be is simply, "Will I get up or won't I?" We cheerfully dedicate "ourselves, our souls and bodies, to be a living sacrifice" at the end of our communion service, but evidently hope this does not apply before breakfast!

My mother once said to me, "Why should I ask God for guidance in the morning? I know what I've got to do in the day." But of course she didn't. Or rather, she knew what she knew, but she didn't know what God knew – who she would meet or who might call, what crises might arise or what opportunities, and indeed whether she should leave the household claims at any point to see a particular person who might be in need, let alone whether the milkman or the cleaning lady might have suffered a bereavement or a family breakdown that day and be in need of counsel and comfort. Even if such things are not always foreseen or warning given, a morning quiet time leaves us in a state of readiness, attuned to God's mind, for the unexpected as well as the expected in the day. The morning is the key. As my father loved to sing in the bathroom in the morning, "Shake off dull sloth, and joyful rise To pay thy morning sacrifice!"

There is an element of wonder in the knowledge that the Creator of all worlds will, from the love which is His nature, communicate with men and women who seek him. This touches something very deep in the nature of man. For as far back as our knowledge of the human race can carry us, we find men who hungered for some deepening contact with the unseen but not unknowable Power behind our universe.

"My soul thirsteth for God, for the living God."

"With my soul have I desired Thee in the night, yea with my spirit within me I will seek Thee early." "My soul thirsteth for Thee, my flesh longeth for Thee in a dry and thirsty land." Men were saying this nearly three thousand years ago. Innumerable others, some known and mostly unrecorded, felt the same way, surely, centuries or millennia earlier in Egypt or in India, on the Euphrates or the Yangtze, among the roving tribes on the plains of North America or among the Aborigines of Australia.

Some may dismiss all this as an example of man's unwillingness to admit that he is alone in a friendless universe, as the personification of our dread of the unknown and our ignorance of the forces of nature around us. To do this, however, is to underestimate the capacity of man, and particularly his faculty of intuitive thinking, "the immediate apprehension, the immediate insight" which at times goes beyond our conscious thinking or our scientifically established knowledge.

I have found that God requires our thinking at its best if we are to find and follow His guidance, and yet in that morning hour there is an understanding that sometimes goes beyond our best thinking. It is different from conscience, which distinguishes right from wrong. It can go beyond rational thought, central as that is to our humanity. It can leap beyond knowledge already acquired to a new insight, carrying a certainty which impels us to act on it. It is like faith, "the evidence of things not seen."

We are dealing, in our apprehension of God, with one of those elements in man which are, it seems, unique. Another goes with it: the apprehension of beauty, which marks a departure in the history of our planet. Who for a moment believes that in all their sixty million years one dinosaur ever admired a sunset? Or plucked one fragrant forest orchid for his mate because it was beautiful? But if man is made in the image of God, it is not unnatural that his inborn powers should lead him into an awareness of God Himself, and into a love of the beauty God has lavished on our world, and doubtless on all worlds, or that men and women should wish to share in something of the nature of God the Creator by creating in their art and music some echo of that beauty.

It is, perhaps, worth emphasising man's difference from the rest of creation since in recent years there has been a tendency to stress his likeness to it. For in his thinking, his imagination, in his creativeness, his art, his technology, to say nothing of the skills of his amazing hands, he is unique. And he alone, as far as we know, reaches out to a Reality beyond the passing cavalcade of life.

If man is qualitatively different from the other inhabitants of earth, perhaps his inner search for contact with the ultimate reality and intelligence of the Person we call God is not to be discounted. Perhaps the most crucial factor now in the evolution of man is that we should learn the secret of that contact on such a scale across the globe that the whole world's life comes to be affected by it far more profoundly than it is at present. This may be one ultimate purpose of the intelligence of man, under the guidance of God.

It is an incomparable experience to be able to spend an hour every morning seeking that attentive contact with the God who loves us; for our minds to be in touch with "the Author of mind". It is the experience of offering to God our highest faculties of thought and imagination, as well as our willingness and obedience, so that He can make known His will for us. It opens up a limitless range of possibilities of what we can be and become and, even more important, what we can enable others to do and be.

The morning hour especially is a time when God pours the peace and refreshment of His presence into our lives. How many people have begun a quiet time jaded or dispirited, as I have done, and have ended an hour later with renewed zest and courage and initiative for the day ahead? It is a time when God's power lifts us like a helicopter above our problems and divisions, our fears and our dullness, into His own dimension of liberty and love.

Whenever my own energies are flagging I like to turn to the bracing company of St. Paul in the morning hour. Paul poured out in his letters his overwhelming belief in the generosity of God, in the magnificence of His calling to us, in His transcendent power to transform human life and make new men and women of us, a new society on earth, a "colony of heaven", through His "utterly dependable" love and support. "He has lifted us right out of the old life," he wrote (he was in prison at the time). He called his friends "God's picked representatives of the new humanity", and summoned them to "be strong, not in yourselves but in the Lord and in the power of His boundless resources", for, he told them, "you hold in your hands the very words of life".

Today, as we find ourselves at this latest page in the long history of the planet, man has been learning through many thousand years of trial, error, growth and toil, to know himself, his earth, something of his universe and a little of the God who sustains the universe. Mankind is coming of age people say, perhaps over-optimistically, and in the view of some this means discarding the idea of God. Yet the highest leap of the human spirit will not fail us here.

Perhaps people do need to discard their inadequate, innocuous, inaccurate or insipid ideas of God. But the idea of God Himself, in love and majesty, is the idea mankind most needs to reach for. Not simply because man may destroy himself in unutterable suffering unless he does, but because this is the true highroad of our evolution. It is what we are made for.

6
Fishers of men

IT WAS December in Berlin, bitterly cold among the ruined buildings still pointing gaunt fingers to the sky. The year: 1956. We were presenting *The Vanishing Island*, Peter Howard's potent and colourful musical, which had just travelled round the world. The huge Titania Palace was crowded out night after night from West and East Berlin – the Wall was not yet built.

One evening I walked into the back of the theatre just as the curtain fell, and stood beside a tall Canadian friend, watching the crowd as they began slowly moving out.

Suddenly a bent, thin, very poorly dressed man turned out of the stream and came towards us. He said hesitantly to my Canadian friend, in English, "Excuse me, but weren't you in Berlin with Dr. Buchman at such and such a hotel in 1936?"

"Why yes," said the Canadian, "I was there. Did we meet then?"

"I was the lift man at the hotel," said the elderly man. "Every day when I took Dr. Buchman up or down in the lift he would talk to me. Once he asked me into his sitting room so that we could talk more freely. I had a terrible problem with drink. My home was breaking up. Dr. Buchman helped me to get free and make a new start. He saved my home. I never forget him."

Then he pulled out a battered old wallet, searched in it and brought out a twenty-year old visiting card. On one side Frank N. D. Buchman, on the other, in Buchman's unmistakable writing, were the words, "To Max, friend and fellow fighter", and his signature. It was moving to see how much it meant to him. The old man thought for a moment. Then he felt in his wallet again and took out a fifty mark note. It looked as if it might be a great deal of all he had.

He handed it to my friend and said, "When you see Dr. Buchman, will you give him this for his work? And will you say to him, 'Max has kept the faith.'"

A moment later he was gone.

I have never forgotten that encounter. To me it reveals the heart of Moral Re-Armament. To Frank Buchman everyone was "a royal soul", and he was as likely to be found giving his deepest truth to the gardener or the cook – or the lift man – as he was to a cabinet minister or an industrialist. In 1936 he had been in Berlin making a last, unsuccessful, attempt to reach at least some of the German leadership with Christ's message of change before it was too late. He failed. He told a Swedish journalist before he left Berlin that "demonic forces" were now at work there. But in the midst of his last bid for pre-war Germany he also met Max – and twenty years later Max had kept the faith.

In his eighties, Frank was once in a Milan hotel, tired and unwell after a long and arduous conference in Caux, and said to a friend of mine who called on him in his room early one morning, "I don't say I'm without sin: I do say I live for one thing only – to make Christ regnant in the life of every person I meet, including the waiter who is just coming to bring me my breakfast." It was the way he always lived and believed all of us should live.

He saw the art of winning men and women as our primary calling. He once said to a friend of mine, as he looked back on his life, "I have been wonderfully led – to those who were ready."

It is often the unexpected person who is ready. A girl in Birmingham read in the press about the leading Gilbert and Sullivan star from Australia, on a visit home to England, who had just announced that he had bought a small Pacific island, off the Great Barrier Reef, to set up an ideal society that all who lived there would enjoy. She felt moved to write to him and say that desert islands would never do it, and what he needed was to find the inner change and peace of heart in his own life which was the key to real living. She recommended a visit to the summer house party of the Oxford Group then in session in Oxford.

Ivan Menzies was the most brilliant and the most impossibly difficult star of the Australian D'Oyly Carte company. Most of his colleagues detested him, which left him wholly untroubled. No one would seem a more unlikely candidate for a radical change of heart. But inwardly Ivan was "ready", something unknown to anyone but himself. His marriage had broken up, and he hungered to find some meaning to life. To the girl's amazement, he turned up at the Oxford house party. It completely changed his life. It was just after this that I first came to know him, the beginning of a friendship which lasted half a century.

Menzies went back to Australia with a consuming passion to give to everyone he could reach, on and off the stage, the marvel of new life God had given him.

The management of the theatre company were alarmed when they heard that Menzies had "got religion". He was bad enough before. When he arrived, Menzies offered to tear up his contract. They decided to continue and see what happened. The result was a triumph from end to end of Australia through the next ten years. His fellow actors found him considerate on stage where before he had always hogged the limelight. He was re-united with his wife Elsie Griffin, herself a great and much loved Gilbert and Sullivan star and with their daughter. And wherever he went he proclaimed his new-found life and helped other people to start. We have met them all over Australia. People were deeply affected in all walks of life, from the Prime Minister of the day to the unemployed or the business set or people in the professions.

I came to know two young teachers, recently married to each other, who, greatly daring, went to talk to him in his dressing room after a performance in Adelaide one night, because of what they had read about him in the press. That talk changed the whole course of their lives, and launched them on a life of service in education and far beyond which has affected many other people and situations over the years.

Ivan's story shows that no one is too "difficult" to find change when the moment comes, and anyone with this experience can share it with other people, or other couples, in such a way that they too can find it for themselves.[1] We can all be led "to those who are ready". In the Acts of the Apostles, Philip is told, Go up to the Gaza road – and so meets the Treasurer to the Queen of Ethiopia, who is "ready", and goes on his way a different man. In Damascus, Ananias is told to call at the house of Judas in Straight Street and speak to Saul of Tarsus. It sounded a recklessly dangerous order. But he went, and out of it came St. Paul and the worldwide Church. Years later in Antioch, the Spirit tells the Christians there, "Set Me apart Barnabas and Saul for the work to which I have called them", and the strategy for winning the Roman Empire begins to unfold, and Saul, using his Roman name Paul, steps into the arena of history.

However the contact comes about, through a thought-out initiative, or the inner conviction to pursue an unexpected encounter, it means laying down our lives alongside the other person's for as long as needful, whether for an hour or a lifetime.

The basis is friendship. No one wants to unburden himself to someone he does not know, or does not trust. And it must be selfless friendship – not being

1. The story is told in *The Song of a Merryman*, London, 1976, by Cliff and Edna Magor – the two young teachers who came to see Ivan Menzies that night in Adelaide in 1935.

friends in order to get someone into our thing. It must be wholly for the other person's sake in order to help him find his own touch with Almighty God.

It also means listening to people, however long it takes. What the other person tells me usually does more to change him than what I tell him. Advice is not what is needed. What he needs is to find his own touch with God himself, whose loved child he is.

A few years ago my wife and I went to stay with a couple in another country, old friends who we knew had been deeply troubled by some events in their lives for the past ten years – not between each other but in relation to certain other people, and their own uncertainty about their calling in life, where they felt they had lost their way. We had not seen them for many years, though we had always kept in touch, and naturally hoped very much to be able to help in some way.

But when we arrived, our clear thought day after day was, "Say nothing. Do the things they would like you to do with them, meet the friends they want you to meet, visit the places they want to take you to, and raise nothing about the past unless they do."

Ten days passed like this. We thoroughly enjoyed ourselves, but several times a day, when we were alone together, we anxiously asked each other if we were missing some crucial opportunity which might never recur. Every time, as we prayed, we were told, "Wait. Say nothing." At the end of ten days we had to go and stay for a week with other friends in the same region, and apparently nothing had happened, although this ten day visit had been one of our main reasons for making a journey half across the world.

At the end of that week we went back to our friends, and as we sat down to supper the husband said, "We just want you to know that we want to be with you in the battle." The log jam had broken without our knowledge. They poured out to us all that had happened in the past ten years, and how they now saw their way forward once again. At last, as we sat together after supper, we had a time of quiet together, when God could shed His illumination on our lives.

After the quiet time, the wife turned to us and said, "All the time you stayed with us, we were struck by the force of the things you did not say."

It was the lesson of a lifetime, which someone like myself, who is always ready with plenty to say, finds it hard to learn. "Who darkens My design with a cloud of thoughtless words?" the voice of God asked Job. We could only be grateful that for once we had known when to be silent and let Him work.

But there are some things that need saying, at the given moment, among them assurance that God has a plan for every life and a way out of every impasse; that light will be shed on life by an honest run down on the standards of honesty, purity, unselfishness and love; that God will guide anyone who will put his or her life squarely into His hands, and give Him space in life every day.

Sometimes it is a strong and direct word that needs to be said – not in reaction or exasperation but in love. On a building site a craggy old plasterer and man of God to the best of his ability, finally felt he must speak straight out to the embittered veteran communist shop steward on the job. "The trouble with you," he said, "is that you're a dictator around here. The men are afraid of you. Come to that, your wife's afraid of you too, and your family. In fact you're the biggest blasted dictator I know. You need the power of God to change you to the roots." Out of the fury that followed came in due time an experience of the revolutionary power of Christ to change a man's life which transformed things on the site and at home, and made the shop steward and his wife a voice for change and a new way of doing things in this and other countries.

"Never talk too big or look too wise", Frank Buchman used to warn us. "Speak up to your own experience and not beyond it". What is real to us in life helps people, not our theories or our sermons. And, "Don't put the hay so high the mules can't get at it." He must have meant this particularly for us in Oxford where we loved to get in the stratosphere when we talked about anything, and where we didn't always stop talking when we'd finished what we had to say.

The great art of winning people seems to come naturally and almost effortlessly to some. To most of us ordinary mortals it probably comes as something we try to learn in practice, over a lifetime. But this is our priority, nevertheless, whatever else we are called to do.

There is a further stage of great importance, too little explored, and that is strategy – God's strategy, not our human planning, to win the men or women in any given situation who will most swiftly and convincingly affect everyone else once their own lives are transformed.

Frank Buchman never tired of giving his favourite illustration of how strategy works: how he went to Pennsylvania State College as a young man, in charge of Christian work there, to find nineteen drunken parties going on the night he arrived, academic work at a low level, the football team losing all its games – and the last person anyone wanted to meet was a Christian worker. His clear guidance in the following days was that three men were the keys to the college, and his strategy was to win them: the tough-hided bootlegger who peddled liquor to the students; an influential student who claimed he was a Confucianist; and the agnostic Dean of the college. The change in these men, one by one, took time, but three years later 1,200 men in the college were doing voluntary Bible study, work had improved and games were being won. Many other lives were affected of course, but it was God's strategy through these three men that turned the tide.[1]

Such strategies have proved the key to industrial disputes, city councils, community problems and sometimes to international situations. It is not that some people are more important than others but that

1. See *The Making of a Miracle* in Buchman's *Remaking the World*. For an account of such a strategy in one South Coast town, see the author's *Reflections on Moral Re-Armament*, London, 1983.

some may hold the key to bringing about God's intentions for everyone more swiftly.

The need to win people to the place of radical change does not stop at the frankly pagan, the interesting sinner, the died-in-the-wool materialist, the confirmed agnostic or the cheerfully immoral. A new lease of life awaits many in the churches, many who have held a sincere faith for many years but are ready for a step forward into a new realm of effectiveness. It may come through finding freedom from binding shackles of compromise or resentment, from a new discipline in setting aside enough time every morning for God to speak to us, or from accepting more fully God's total demands on our lives. It may come from a simple willingness to go out to people in a new way.

Often our effectiveness in helping someone else comes from a readiness to make some simple sacrifice in our own lives. Once in New Zealand we got to know an outstanding Maori woman at a conference we were attending. She did a devoted work caring for young Maori drug addicts in her home town. We also noticed that she herself was a compulsive chain smoker, barely able to survive a meal or a meeting without lighting up. One day I had the thought to ask her, "Do you think you might be able help your young addicts more if you weren't addicted to smoking yourself?" "Oh!" she said, "you sound just like my husband!" Then she added, "To tell you the truth, I had the same thought myself this morning." Over alcohol it was this pastoral issue which finally weighed with me, the growing conviction that to help anyone with an addiction I need to live free of any addiction myself, even a moderate one. It is not much help to say to an alcoholic, "You ought to be a moderate drinker like me". What he, or she, needs to hear is, "God can give you complete liberty never to touch another drop, and I know because that is how I live myself."

Whatever else we aim to do, this work of bringing Christ's revolution into the lives of people is basic. This was the missing factor in Eastern Europe for forty years and in the Soviet Union for much longer, the experience the communist world so direly lacked. Those who took power believed with Marx and Lenin that materialism is the supreme and only truth. "Our morality is subordinate to the class struggle," said Lenin.

In consequence they rejected the power of God to change recalcitrant human nature, in themselves or anyone else. So their leadership ended, in country after country, in a self-perpetuating, tyrannical mafia who ruled by the secret police and mercilessly robbed the very peoples they claimed to liberate. In the end they were swept away in a matter of months.

The urgent question now is how to establish swiftly enough the faith and moral values on which lasting freedom and democracy can be built. And to be sure we are doing the same in our own materially motivated societies.

7
Husband and wife are one . . . ?

IN THE late 1930's I worked for four years in the South of England with an old friend, Peter Phelps. Peter was one of the men I had come to know in the first days after my decision in Oxford. His lodgings were near to mine and we used to meet daily. He helped greatly to stabilise me in my new found faith. He was a little senior to me, and already wise in understanding the ways of God to man.

Peter's natural inclination, I think, would have been to become a cricketing bishop. He could hit any kind of ball, on the golf course or elsewhere, with daunting accuracy. He played cricket for the Oxford University Authentics, and for his home county, Worcestershire, on the most beautiful cricket ground in the world. He was also heading for a theological college (at Cambridge, broadmindedly). But after that God had other revolutionary plans for him, and he rendered far-reaching service in many parts of the world. He was a man of immense integrity and courage, and a great sense of humour. He also put up patiently with my impatience and brashness, and I learned a great deal from him through the years we worked together. I never managed to beat him at golf, even when he gave a a stroke a hole. Those years in the South of England were a creative, fruitful and non-stop time, and we enjoyed them immensely.

Our work was to support the hundreds of people in the Oxford Group throughout the Southern counties. They came from all walks of life and were firm friends, from Harry, who ran the fruit barrow on a Bognor Regis housing estate, and George the bricklayer in Eastbourne to men and women in business and the professions, in civic life, and, of course, in any number of homes. One staunch friend was the Assistant Chief Constable of his county. Another, editor of a daily newspaper, could only be visited after one o'clock in the morning, when the paper had been put to bed and he could relax, so Peter and I had some short nights in consequence. Most of them were in demanding jobs or home making, which limited the time they had available. We were footloose and so could help carry through the events, large or small, which they wanted to set in motion, in addition to the ones we initiated ourselves.

We based our operations on fifty homes between Kent and Cornwall, where we were always welcome. They were a most varied group of families: a doctor in Folkestone, a school master in Horsham, a vicar in Eastbourne, a retired RAF couple in Brighton, a portrait photographer in Bognor Regis, a town councillor in Winchester, a woman magistrate in Torquay and many more. Everyone of them had a varied team building up around them and were always reaching out to other people.

Often the different teams met weekly, and sometimes we held regional gatherings as well – from

HUSBAND AND WIFE ARE ONE . . . ?

Sussex, for instance, on John Meekings' farm at Bolney, surrounded by his 42,000 hens – and we did our best to help set in motion fresh ways to reach other people so that they might try the experiments that could lead them to the heart of Christian faith. We had large public meetings on many occasions over the four years we worked there – Horsham drill hall, the de la Warr pavilion in Bexhill, theatres in Bournemouth and Bognor Regis, the Dorking Halls, and innumerable smaller occasions in hotels, town halls, churches and homes. We occasionally gathered the work of previous months together in a House Party somewhere, to enlist and train new people.

They were arduous and rewarding years. We travelled constantly, in the black and red second-hand Standard which was given to us by a director of a motor company in Bournemouth. Our work was always with people, with our own teams and their friends, and also with civic leaders, Members of Parliament, editors of newspapers and many others whom we came to know over the years. On the eve of war, in June 1939, we gathered much of this together through a day in the Pavilion in Bognor Regis, then the largest covered floor space in the South of England, where 4,000 people took part from all over the South, on the theme "Moral Re-Armament the strength of citizenship."

I should add that we were within reach of golf courses wherever we went, and tried to put in a round or two each week. When war broke out we made for the course at Pulborough which we regarded as the best in the South of England, and played a ceremonial round, with RAF planes droning ceaselessly overhead to France, in case it should prove to be our last before we were called up!

One of the interesting friends Peter and I worked with was Lionel Exton, Chairman of the Exton chain of hotels in and around Bournemouth and of the prestigious Palace Court Hotel, and director of numerous other enterprises from the ice rink to the ice-cream factory, from major motor companies to the leading fruit and vegetable suppliers.

In the early 'thirties Leo and his wife had three small children, Leone, Clive and Valerie who were at a pre-school class run by Gweneth Medwin in a large room in her parents' home in Westbourne. Gweneth met the Oxford Group at this time and life for her was transformed. She learned to listen to God daily, and told the children about it. One day Leone, the eldest of the three, asked her, "Miss Medwin, can children listen to God too?" So she began to have times of quiet with the whole class, and they often shared together the thoughts that came to them. One day Clive had the thought, "Eat up your food". It sounds unusual for a growing boy, but his reluctance and slowness in eating caused his mother constant anxiety.

Before long Mrs. Exton was round at the school in a high state of excitement. "What have you done to Clive?" she asked. "He's started to eat up his food." It was not long before she too began to base her life on finding and following God's will day by day. But her husband had no wish to be mixed up in that kind of thing.

However she persisted, and some time later when they had to go on a visit to Suffolk she persuaded him to drive back via Oxford, where the Oxford Group house party was taking place. "Well, just one night and no more" decreed Leo. They sat in a meeting in Lady Margaret Hall and listened to the speakers. Towards the end the leader of the meeting suggested they should all have some moments of quiet and ask if God had any thoughts for them, and advised them to write down any such thoughts if they came. Leo, very self-consciously, scribbled into his diary the only thought that came to him: "You cannot serve God and Mammon".

This was the turning point of his life. He had done pretty well by Mammon so far, but from this moment on he lived to find and follow God's plan for his life. I have seldom known anyone as single-minded as Leo was for the rest of his days.

This began to have an effect in many directions in the town and in the way the hotels were run. Over the next years he overhauled his whole idea of how to care for staff and run the business. He eventually helped and encouraged the men who were trying to form the first union for hotel workers just before the war.

One day Richard Harman, owner of a group of trade journals, one of which was for the hotel business, came down to Bournemouth in search of copy for it. He went into a barber's shop to have his hair cut and began talking to the man in the next chair who he found was working in a hotel. "What are things like where you work?" he asked, expecting the usual tale of woe about poor pay and conditions. "Well," said the man, "where I work conditions are fine, the pay is all right and the management is very considerate towards us." "Where on earth do you work?" Harman asked. "Oh, I work for Mr. Exton at Linden Hall Hydro," said the man.

Within the hour Harman was in the foyer at Linden Hall talking to Leo Exton. Peter and I happened to be there too and watched with interest. Harman said, "Would you write me an article on personnel management?" Exton replied, "You know, all I've learned about that comes from my meeting the Oxford Group. Now next weekend they've got a conference at Eastbourne. Why don't you come along there with me and then perhaps we can do the article together afterwards."

That weekend changed the whole course of Harman's life and led to thirty years of creative and imaginative publishing by Blandford Press, including books which carried the faith he had now found far and wide across the world.

Of course Leo Exton's change had its effects in the family. His sister, Winifred Foss, was manager at Linden Hall. Tough, atheist, with a broken marriage behind her, she became almost unrecognisable when the love of God broke into her life. It affected everything she did. It also affected her three high-powered sons: Patrick, regular officer in the RAF, Hannen, then running an advertising agency, and Denis, largest and toughest, trained for the Merchant Navy.

HUSBAND AND WIFE ARE ONE . . . ?

One by one over the years, each one found the same experience: Denis first, when he came to break up an Oxford Group meeting and stayed to listen. He had some hectic years in the Merchant Navy through the war, and then was a very experienced ship's Captain for many years until retirement, and is now a publisher. Hannen became a brilliant film maker and photographer, much loved at the BBC. And Pat, the last to change, had a dangerous and distinguished war service, and was finally decorated for his outstanding work in building up Transport Command.[1]

There are of course endless ramifications of this one family's influence. Their story is typical of so many people in every walk of life with whom Peter and I were privileged to work in those years.

At one point, late in 1937, however, I had felt dissatisfied with the effectiveness of what we were doing. Something fresh seemed called for, but I did not know what. I was on my own for a day or two, and staying in Bournemouth as the guest of Lionel Exton in one of his hotels. Peter was in one of the other Southern towns for some days and we were due to join up again shortly.

One night I determined I would not go to bed till I had found from the Almighty some fresh light on our work, if He would give it me. For four hours in my hotel room I prayed, listened, read the New Testament and pondered. Half way through this

---

1. See *Climbing Turns, A Pilot's Story in Peace and War*, by Group Captain Patrick Foss, OBE, Linden Hall, 1990.

marathon a thought came clearly into my mind which had nothing whatever to do with what I was thinking about, and I wrote it down: "Admit you are in love with Stella". "Well," I thought to myself, "so I am", and returned to the business in hand. My composure was to be short-lived.

Stella Corderoy met the Oxford Group in the same year as I did. She came to the Oxford House Party that year to protect her mother who had been invited there, but like the young lady of Riga came back inside the tiger. She came from a well-known Methodist family, became an atheist, regained her faith through a Presbyterian preacher and was confirmed in the Church of England. She was, when she came to the house party, the school social worker at St. Michael's, Chester Square, in the days of Canon Elliott, "the radio parson". She had a very good mind, was remarkably beautiful and was a fantastically good cook. I came to know her and her family when we were both working together at our London headquarters in the mid-'thirties.

In the summer of 1937 her mother invited me to join them on holiday in Austria for three weeks as companion to her younger brother Oliver. (Their father died when Stella was eleven, and the elder brothers had long since left home). One or two of my more realistic friends warned me that proximity of this sort would probably mean I should return thinking I was in love with Stella. I determined to show them that I did not fall for anyone as easily as that and returned, as I thought, heart-whole. Hence the word "admit" in my guidance that night three months later. Men, as is well known, are hopeless at knowing what is going on inside them, and clearly the Almighty was better informed about myself than I was.

That was in December. In January the full force of the situation hit me like a tidal wave, and I was swept away on the flood. So much so that some weeks later when I managed to get up to London on one of my infrequent visits, I slipped off one morning without saying a word to anyone and proposed to her. Stella, who thought she was probably in love with someone else at the time, turned me down gently but adamantly, and my world lay in ruins.

I had, of course, broken the first law of fellowship. I had acted completely unilaterally in a matter of major consequence not only to Stella and myself, but to the colleague I was working with and to our fellowship as a whole. I had not had the common sense, let alone the common courtesy, to consult and seek guidance with any of my close friends on whether this was the right moment, before taking such a momentous step. The result was catastrophe. My original thought may indeed have been from God. My precipitate, self-willed action was not.

The painful months that followed led to a searching but therapeutic review of my life and my motives, throwing into sharp focus both my self-willed determination to get my own way and my readiness to sacrifice any other consideration for something I wanted really badly. It showed up the immaturity of my whole approach to marriage. It may indeed have been the marriage God had in mind for us, but equally clearly I was not yet marriageable till further deep changes had taken place in my character.

It came home to me in those months that what I really needed saving from by Jesus Christ was not just the things I did wrong, which were numerous, but the fact that I myself was wrong, and that until I had yielded that central citadel of self to Him more deeply than ever before, I would always be involved in wrong actions however hard I tried to do the right ones. What made me feel worst of all was the fear that I had messed up Stella's life as well as my own by not having the grace to wait on God's timing, so that I had disrupted what I still felt was His plan for us.

Though the following months were rough inwardly, they were also full and productive in our work, including the launching of Moral Re-Armament[1] in June, 1938, and Peter and I were developing campaigns throughout the South of England. There was so much to do and so many people to reach that I had no time to brood, though the pain persisted unabated. Eighteen months after my proposal we were at war.

One thing I was sure of as time went by: if I could not marry Stella I would never marry anyone. My father took considerable exception to this attitude which he thought unreasonable for a young man still in his twenties. He did not really know Stella, however, and at one point during the war, when he was preaching in Liverpool, he invited himself over

1. See Chapter eight.

to our evacuation headquarters in Cheshire where Stella was working, to see what she was like. He wrote me afterwards, "I have seen Stella, and I think you are absolutely right", which says a lot for his perception and largeness of heart.

The war came to an end eventually and we began to be demobilised. A dozen of us who were just out of the Services spent a week together at our Cheshire centre seeking God's mind on where our work was meant to go and where each one of us was meant to throw his weight. By this time Stella had returned to London. One day, at the end of a long afternoon by myself out of doors, God spoke plainly: "Take on the literature of the work." This was a moment when there was a great demand for our books and we had some first rate writers in the field. Peter Howard's first three books had sold half a million copies during the war, and more were on the way. This was clearly an area of great potential expansion. It also called for the urgent mastery of professional skills because of the sheer impossibility of getting anything printed or published in the aftermath of war.

My colleagues agreed that I was on the right track, and I headed back to London. I assumed I would be working with my old friend Raymond Nelson, who had been President of the University Dance Band in our youth, and who had brilliantly carried our literature through the war years while doing a full-time job as an officer in the National Fire Service.

I found two complications when I arrived. The first was that Ray Nelson had bowed out of our literature altogether in order to take on the complex travel arrangements for moving large forces of Moral Re-Armament across war-devastated Europe.

The second, much more alarming, was that while I was in Cheshire a similar meeting had been going on in London, where the future handling of our literature had been raised. One person there had felt impelled to take it on: Stella. She too thought she would be working with Nelson. The person she found she would be working with was me!

I suppose Providence has a sense of humour, though it didn't strike either of us as particularly funny at the time. Stella was convinced I would want to run the show and treat her as my secretary, and she meant to be a principal or nothing. And I said to myself, "What if the tiger gets out of the cold room?" A peculiar metaphor, but you see what I mean. I was pretty accustomed by now, if hardly reconciled, to a life without Stella, but what might happen to my feelings when I was working closely with her every day of the week?

My guidance as I thought about it was that there was only one thing to do, and that was to play absolutely fair. It was up to me not to show by the flicker of an eyelid or a tone of voice that I was still in love with her, never to be on the make for myself in any way as we worked together. If I did, it would be intolerable for her and our work would suffer, and that was really more important than anything I might be feeling. There were times when this drove me to my knees at intervals through the day, but it worked.

There followed a remarkable year together, including some feats of publishing I can't go into here, and in the course of which Stella personally piloted through the publication and distribution of 1,100,000 copies of a booklet aimed at heightening industrial teamwork, sound homes and unity in the nation, based on faith in God, as we faced the post-war years.

Throughout this time I had no guidance of any kind to reconsider my position with Stella. We were close colleagues, we enjoyed working together, and that was all. And indeed, throughout that year it would have been fruitless to do so, because on that issue her attitude to me remained unchanged.

Others however were observant. We had a wonderful group of cleaning ladies in our London centre, and when they met for mid-morning tea they sometimes discussed the marital prospects of the young people they met there. One morning, one of them said she thought Mr. So-and-so was going to be the one for Miss Stella. "No, no!" said Mrs. Letts, the head cleaning lady, a devout Catholic and a great friend to us all. "No, no. Not him. It's Mr. Ken. You should see the way he looks at Miss Stella when she passes the open door of his office. He's the one!" So much for my discretion.

Something, however was happening at a deeper level, and one day, on top of a bus, Stella realised she was in love with me and wanted more than anything for us to marry.

She consulted a close friend to ask if she ought to give me some indication of her change of attitude after all these years. When they sought guidance together, her friend wisely said, "If this is what God

wants He will tell Ken. If not, it isn't right anyway."
So Stella laid her feelings in God's hands and prepared
to await the event in patience and also in gratitude,
whether it came to fruition or not. Of course, I knew
nothing of all this.

Five days later we were at a meeting in our headquarters. At one point I looked across the room to where Stella was sitting beside her brother Oliver, still in uniform. As I did so, God spoke with crystal clarity: "It is right. The time has come." It was His first word of this sort for eight years.

My first reaction after the meeting was panic. Could I really risk everything again and perhaps suffer a second, and irretrievable, rebuff? Dare I really start it all up again? But my conviction was clear, and this time I would make no mistake by launching out precipitately. There were three of my colleagues who knew us both extremely well who I felt I must talk it over with. They could be relied on for candid judgment. I did so, one by one, and they all agreed it was right for me to try. Then I went to see Frank Buchman who was in London. It was the afternoon of V-Day, 1946, and Stella and Oliver and I had watched the parades in the Mall all morning.

Buchman was having his tea in bed. He was nearly seventy and had had a severe stroke during the war. But he was more alert than ever mentally, and took a lively interest in all of us. I felt I owed it to him to share my conviction that I should marry one of his choicest whole-time workers.

"Well, Ken", he said cheerfully as I sat beside his

bed, "what's on your mind?" I told him as best I could.

"How long have you felt this way about each other?" he asked.

"Well, Frank", I said "I've felt this way for a good many years but I haven't any idea what Stella feels."

Buchman munched a piece of cake and considered this briefly. "Well," he said, "that's the first thing you'll have to ask her, isn't it?" Then after a moment he added, "I'm sure she'll have you", which cheered me greatly.

Then he said, "Let's have a quiet time", and we listened together.

"What came to you?" he asked after a while, and I read out what I had written down.

"Do you mean to tell me," he asked quizzically, "that you have guidance you should get engaged?"

"Yes, Frank, I have."

"So have I," beamed Buchman, "underscored three times!" (He always underlined his most emphatic guidance like this.)

"Where is she now?" he asked, looking rather like a schoolboy up to mischief. "Can you ask her tonight?" And then, always a realist, "Have you got any money?"

I reassured him on all points and then, as I was about to go, I asked him "Can we pray together Frank?"

"Oh, I would like that," he said. So he prayed, and then I prayed, and then he prayed again, and each time he prayed he repeated a verse from one of his favourite hymns:

> Sweet the moments, rich in blessing,
> Which before Thy Cross I spend,
> Life and health and peace possessing
> From the sinner's dying Friend.

I had never heard it before and have never forgotten it since. Some might think this an unusual note on which to send a young man out on such a mission. But Buchman knew that if Stella said Yes, many sweet moments would come our way and plenty of hard ones too as life went by, so he was pointing us to where true joys and true satisfaction are to be found. He was offering us a gift for the whole of our married life, and I shall always be grateful.

So I took my leave and set out to find Stella. We came back to him a couple of hours later. Stella gave him a kiss and he looked at us benignly, "There's been too much of this British austerity, far too much," he said. After an interminably long engagement of five weeks we were married at St. Mark's, Hamilton Terrace and lived happily ever after.

All this goes to show that it isn't easy even for our worst mistakes to frustrate God's plan indefinitely, even if it takes a bit of time to bring it about, and perhaps it wouldn't have taken quite so long in our case if a world war hadn't intervened. We were both in our mid-thirties when Frank Buchman gave us the blessing at the end of our wedding service. A bit late starting, some might think, but it made our hard-won love all the more precious and all the more durable, and we were both much easier people to live with than we would have been if it had happened earlier! Our daughter, son and daughter-in-law celebrated our 40th wedding anniversary superbly a few years ago.

At our wedding in 1946, Stella, on her brother George Corderoy's arm, came into the church to the singing of the hymn "Praise the Lord, ye heavens adore Him". Two lines from that hymn have been a watchword for me ever since:

> Praise the Lord for He is glorious,
> *Never* shall His promise fail.

We had of course to learn a good many more things along the road. Some of these we collected a few years ago in a talk we gave in the Church hall in our village, entitled "Husband and wife are one – but which one?" It has since been published as a booklet.[1] Its title recalls medieval French law which, as Stella often told me disapprovingly in our early married life, ruled that "husband and wife are one and that one is the husband"! Not quite the note to strike today. So in our talk we explored decision making and who is right in family life, and the uniting effect when we decide it is not a question of what father says, or what mother says, or what the children say, but what God says that settles the issues.

One of the points we touched on is the lethal danger of coming to marriage for what you can get out of it, especially if you come with any demands beginning, "I have a right to . . ." As we point out, in marriage it doesn't take many rights to make it go

---

1. Published by Grosvenor Books, London, 1982.

wrong. The supreme safeguard of a marriage is to have Christ as the unseen third partner, so that the alliance is entered into because He wants it and is lived for His outward-looking aims. Then its durability depends on His power and love, not on the fluctuating temperaments of two strong-willed people, each trying to get what they want for themselves.

A friend wrote me recently and said that a line that had meant a lot to him in a recent book of mine was where I spoke of "the riches and pleasures of permanence in the lifelong partnership of two maturing people", something so lamentably, missing in the come-and-go marriages of today, serial and short-lived because they often get off to the wrong start. They are like the traveller who asked the Irishman, "Is this the way to Ballybunion?" To which the Irishman replied, "If I wanted to get to Ballybunion, I wouldn't be starting from here." So many marriages start from the wrong place under the multitudinous pressures of modern life, however good their intentions. Sometimes the lessons are taken to heart, which probably explains why second marriages sometimes succeed where first ones did not, because they are entered into more thoughtfully and realistically. But it is a fearful price to pay, especially for the children.

Another point we touched on in our talk which seems to me fundamental yet seldom mentioned, is that in marriage we should never expect from each other what only God can give. That deep, inarticulate yearning in all of us for reality often gets directed to a person when it is really a search for God Himself, and He alone can satisfy it. "Our souls are restless till they rest in Thee."

We are all finite people and prone to get things wrong, very human sinners as often as not. He is the source of the energy of love we enjoy from Him and need to have constantly renewed for each other. Nor need we be unduly daunted by our shortcomings. That can just be hurt pride instead of simple realism. And, as Julian of Norwich so luminously says, "Our falling hindereth Him not to love us."

If we bank on the divine love, He will give us all we need for ourselves and for each other. I am not what Stella most deeply needs. Christ is, and sometimes, though by no means always, He may give what He wants to give her through me, or to me through her. It is a high privilege and trust we hold for each other.

The hour of the morning quiet time is a mighty bastion of family life. It means we start the day at peace in God and with each other. We can keep short accounts: any rubs and difficulties are liquidated instantly. It means we move in step even if the day takes us far apart, because we not only know what each other is doing, but also what each of us is most deeply feeling – hopes, fears, frustrations, whatever it may be, and can pray for each other and give each other mutual support. It means that we tackle the day, the known and the unknown, with free hearts and minds ready to give our best to whoever or whatever we encounter.

Today, as we grow older, our daily need, more

than ever, is that hour of quiet each morning before the living God.

8
Pilgrims of the impossible

> Got any rivers you say are impassable?
> Got any mountains you can't tunnel through?
> We specialise in the wholly impossible,
> Doing the things that no man can do.
> *Song of the Panama Engineers*

"Pilgrims of the Impossible" is the title of one of my father's books and it is a fair description of the task we are all called to in the world. Though my father, who quoted the Song of the Panama Engineers in the book, would have been the first to affirm that the impossible often becomes possible when the factor of faith enters in.

As men and women of faith we are faced with a formidable task: how to bring a new way of doing things, a new set of values, a new programme of life, and new goals for social and economic well-being to the 4,000 million people on our planet, millions of whom seem to maintain a high level of cruelty and violence, exploitation and aggression.

One trouble is that it is never the same 4,000 million two weeks running. It is like standing beside a never-ending, fast-moving conveyor belt trying to sort out myriads of components as it speeds along. "Time like an ever-rolling stream bears all its sons away", and its daughters too. No sooner have you won your victories than they are whirled away remorselessly and you have to begin again. Before too long you are whirled away yourself. Of course there is a massive overlap, but not enough for us ever to say, "Thank God, the job is done."

But this is no reason for failing to come to grips with our contemporary world. The battle has to be fought and won – or lost – in every generation, and no one can say that any stage of the process is unimportant. The new type of man we need is not hereditary. You can't bequeath a new quality of life, and you can't inherit it till you have already found it. But you can do your best to demonstrate it and encourage the coming generations to try it for themselves. If you do this they may carry it further than you have done.

We need to keep a true perspective on the battle we have to fight. It is all too easy to foreshorten time, and we can fall into a false euphoria when things are going well, and a false despair when they are not. I have heard people say, "I want to see the world won in my lifetime," which may be meant as a spur to the laggards but is hardly a picture of reality. However high our expectations, the magnitude of the task may escape us, just as the hand-wringing attitude of "we never lived in such terrible times", which people have felt in every age, may paralyse us unnecessarily.

God after all is the Master of time. He created it. As the small girl said, "God made time so everything wouldn't happen at once." Whatever His reasons, it is the reality in which we live as long as we are on the earth, and we may as well try to learn His lessons from it.

One, certainly, is the scale and continuity of this battle for the thinking and living of the human race.

It is easy to fall in love with prototypes. This is the trap into which some of the great American evangelists of the nineteenth century, like Charles Finney, fell: they were so sure that people were being won to Christ at such a rate, which seemed to be ever increasing, that there was no need to formulate any programme of social change because all that would take care of itself. This is a dangerous half-truth, because while social change without a change in people may at times be ineffective, the assumption that a change in people will automatically lead to social change may result in the needless perpetuation of injustice.

Some miracles of God in a person's life, or a nation's, are so startling, so far-reaching in their effect on an industry or an international situation or whatever it may be, that we exclaim, rejoicing, "This is the answer!" Well, so it is: a new era of human relations, the future development of man, a fresh way of living for a disordered world, the hope of generations to come, may be implicit in it, and nothing should undervalue it. And yet – it is still a prototype that has yet to go into production, however great its promise, and this is what we must bend our minds to.

My friend Reggie Owbridge, who was at Cambridge when I was at Oxford, helped to build the first Spitfire. He worked at Supermarine, near Southampton, and helped construct the prototype. It would be legitimate to say that the winning of the Battle of Britain was implicit in that first Spitfire, that the victory was already won because that one plane existed. But we also know that the battle would never have been won at all without a prodigious, brilliant and sustained level of production all over the country – aluminium saucepans, Lord Beaverbrook, the Ministry of Aircraft Production and all, to say nothing of the pilots who flew the planes and the ground crews who kept them in the air.

So as men and women of faith we have to think how to multiply what we know to be true in our own lives and other peoples', on a large enough scale to have an effect on the life of the world. The fact that we ourselves may seem to be living and working in some apparently unimportant corner should not daunt us or limit our expectations of where God can lead us.

The worse thing would be for us to get narrowed down to some kind of holding operation, just because of the magnitude of the task.

Nothing would seem further from the intentions of Jesus Christ who proclaimed that the Reign of God has begun, that the Kingdom is already among us, in this world, now. And whatever some people may say, His criterion of judgment does not seem to have been whether or not people said "Jesus is Lord", but whether they fed the hungry, visited the prisoners, clothed the naked, cared for the sick, for His sake. It sounds uncomfortably like what some people pejoratively call the social gospel. At any rate it is plain that He looked for the incarnation of love in action, not in words alone. Clearly, as the Sermon on the Mount and so much more of Jesus' teaching makes evident, what he intended was a new order of human relationships growing out of new men and women, and reaching their most practical as well as their most spiritual needs. The tragedy is that so many who called themselves Christian have signally failed to live like this down the centuries.

We all tend, I believe, to underestimate God's time-scale of history and think of it too much in terms of our short human life-span. From that standpoint 2,000 years is a long time. A thousand years ago they thought in the same way, and as the year 1,000 AD dawned, hill tops across Europe were crowded with people waiting to see the end of the world.

But of course, on the time-scale of the universe such periods are almost too short to measure. Man is in his infancy. According to the scientists it took 4,500 million years before the world and the human race were ready for God's revelation of Himself in Jesus Christ. Against the almost unimaginable length of geological time, the story of man, as I once read, is a footnote to the last page of the last book in a library. Measured in human effort and suffering, every year of man's history seems too long. Measured against the history of our world, a thousand years is a fraction of a moment of time. And even if the pace is quickening as man begins to take command of his own evolution and accelerates his mastery of the material world, there is still an untold future in front of him. If God needs another 100,000 years to work out His purposes for the human race, or another 100 million, that would not be surprising. At the present rate of progress, even if we succeed in not destroying ourselves with our own inventions, it seems likely to take a good long time. We had better settle down to tackling the situation as systematically as we can and to ensuring that generations to come will take up the opportunity He offers and carry it to new horizons.

God has a plan for every man and woman. We are called to serve Him in a thousand million places and professions, in homes, factories, coal mines, hospitals, cabinets, farms, schools, or wherever it may be. What matters is that He calls us to whatever we do with our lives.

The ending of the Second World War opened up new horizons for people in every continent. Not only was there a vast work of reconciliation to be done, but countries across Asia and Africa and elsewhere were in the throes of moving to independence. At the same time, industries had to be renewed throughout the recently warring nations, while communism was militantly reaching out to every part of the globe.

In 1938, in East London, Frank Buchman had launched his call for moral and spiritual re-armament as the nations were re-arming and seemed to be moving inexorably to war. His call was for immediate action by everyone who would rise to it. He ended, "We have not yet tapped the great creative sources in the Mind of God. . . . We can, we must and we will generate a moral and spiritual force that is powerful enough to remake the world."[1] The response was instant and worldwide.

Peter and I ran meetings on it and wrote articles for the press throughout the South of England. The "Sussex Daily News" published seventeen centre page feature articles of mine in the following twelve months. In September we took 300 people from the South to the first World Assembly for Moral Re-Armament at Interlaken, in Switzerland. Frank Buchman, who addressed the Assembly repeatedly, was trying to reach out through press and radio to the men who held the decisions in their hands, as well as to the audiences in front of him. He was also trying to prepare us for what lay ahead:

"Humanity is at the crossroads. Do we choose the road of selfishness that leads to uncontrollable violence and darkness? Or will it be the road of the Cross to a sound world, where we learn how to live together, where the ancient virtues of justice, understanding and peace rule under God over a sane humanity?. . . . Where are the men in every land who will rise and accept the sovereignty of the living God and who will answer the aching hunger of mankind for peace and a new world?"

After the Assembly we spent some days in Geneva where Carl Hambro chaired a lunch for five hundred diplomats and delegates to the League of Nations,

---

1. This and other quotations are from *Remaking the World*, the collected speeches of Frank N. D. Buchman, London, 1961

with Buchman as chief guest. I was, very briefly, one of the speakers – no doubt for the younger generation! A friend then asked me to drive his car back to London, via Ostend, as he was called away elsewhere. Another friend, Ken Noad, and I set out in this small Ford, up the line of the old Western front of World War I. It was the week before Munich. We passed fields of autumn crocus. We also passed one after another of the vast war cemeteries. At one place an old tank stood, set in concrete as a reminder. France was mobilising. In every village men called up were making their way to the railway stations. In Laon, where we spent the night, the troop trains ran incessantly. It seemed incredible that it might all begin again. In Bruges, where we stopped for lunch, we decided to drive out to the gallery where the glorious Memlings were displayed, in case we never lived, or they never survived, to see them again.

A year later, not long after the war began, Frank, who had been launching Moral Re-Armament nationwide in North America, cabled to some of us meeting in London: "Remember, when doubts and difficulties occur, the temptation is always to do lesser things and take a lesser course. But we must never forget that we are called to be remakers of the world." I often thought of it in the years that followed.

Our experiences through the six years of war were a striking vindication to pilgrims of the impossible, and on a far greater scale than we had imagined. They led to a new dimension of faith and our understanding of the values of the Spirit. The guidance of

God could not be rationed, and was an ever present light through danger and difficulty. At one point in 1940, when France was falling and the assault on Britain was imminent, I wrote the following lines,[1]

> . . . So much has lost all meaning in this hour
> That, bold as pylons on a starlit sky,
> The few unshaken certainties stand strong.
> In the last poverty of loss and pain
> These stand secure, and we at length have found
> The eternal riches, the eternal power,
> The ultimate essentials which endure.
> There is a freedom on the frontiers of our days,
> And wealth past all belief in losing all.
> Courage and friends and faith,
> These, these remain; and Christ is over all.
> What more can any man ask
> From life or death?

We all realised that our battle was to sustain the spirit of our own country till victory was won, but beyond that to reach out worldwide to find the men and women who would live to rebuild the post-war world. Nearly all our whole-time workers were called up and a number gave their lives and are sorely missed to this day. I was called up into the newly formed National Fire Service, and found myself fighting fires caused by enemy bombing in South coast ports, till I was transferred to London. After some months I was posted to assist the head of the

---

1. From *We Build a City*, 1990

administration of our Division, which looked after the Houses of Parliament, Westminster Abbey, Buckingham Palace, Victoria station and much else besides, from our headquarters in Dean's Yard, Westminster.

We lived through the Battle of Britain, the blitz on London, massive disasters overseas, the flying bombs and rockets, and the gathering momentum of response before D-Day and beyond.

We received great numbers of service men and women from all over the world at the London headquarters of MRA, and kept in touch as best we could with the outside world. I edited and wrote a Service newsletter which went out to three thousand of our friends in the services on the front lines and elsewhere, aimed at feeding their faith and encouraging them with news of what their comrades were doing, as far as it could be safely described, with initials but no names mentioned. I often wrote the newsletters in the lunch hour at my NFS HQ.

We might seem cut off from each other's countries by the war, and unable to travel, but in fact the message and strategy of Moral Re-Armament were carried round the world by men and women in the services, who turned up in the most remarkable places and took action there, whatever their rank or lack of it. One old Oxford friend of mine, Harry Fletcher who was in the Army in North Africa, found himself appointed Mayor of Benghazi in the latter part of the war. Intelligence sources warned that on a certain day there was going to be open conflict (for reasons I no longer remember) between Arabs and

Jews across North Africa. So Harry went to work in Benghazi, befriending and talking with the leaders of both sides. On the day the expected clashes broke out elsewhere, he had them all together at a tea party at his headquarters, discussing with him how they could create better understanding between their communities!

Our links with Frank Buchman in America were made possible by men who went to and fro across the Atlantic in the line of duty in the different services, including Rear-Admiral Sir Edward Cochrane, Commodore of Convoys in the North Atlantic, and Barty Bostell, whose rank was minimal, but who made frequent crossings, and who, sadly, finally lost his life when his ship went down.

There were so many extraordinary stories of men's lives preserved through the promptings of guidance. Wing-Commander Edward Howell's story from Crete and Greece was so remarkable that as soon as he was fit enough to be flown back from Egypt to London, he had to go and tell it personally to Churchill. His book about it is not to be missed.[1]

It is no wonder that when the war ended and men and women started to be demobilised, or were able to leave key civilian posts in factories and mines and elsewhere, we should all share an over-mastering desire to do whatever might be asked of us to affect the future.

At this moment our comrades in Switzerland, who

1. *Escape to Live*, by Edward Howell, London, 1947.

had been almost totally cut off by the war, took an immensely courageous and sacrificial decision: to buy and equip a centre in Switzerland which would be at the disposal of Frank Buchman and Moral Re-Armament, with the aim of healing the hurts and divisions of the war worldwide, as a contribution to creating a different future in the turmoil of the post-war world.

"Mountain House", the old Caux Palace, is a vast hotel, perched 2,000 feet above Montreux, on the Lake of Geneva, (3,000 feet above sea level). It was derelict and took monumental persistence and work to get it into shape. A hundred Swiss people pulled out of their jobs to help, and many gave their savings or sold their chalets to raise the money. Soon three other hotels were added, giving us 1,000 beds in Caux. Sometimes half as many beds again were in use, from Montreux and Glion below to the Rochers de Naye 3,000 feet above, during the Assemblies that ran from June to October every year.

We were affected in a very direct way. Frank Buchman gave the blessing at our wedding in London one Saturday in July, 1946, and three days later opened Caux for the first time. Ten days after that we arrived there from our Swiss honeymoon. A year later I was asked to go for some weeks to Switzerland to advise on a publishing project our Swiss friends had in mind. The project proved impracticable at that moment, but one result was that I got to know our Swiss colleagues, who were carrying such heavy loads, much more fully. Shortly afterwards, Stella and I and our seven month old daughter were pressingly invited to move to Switzerland and help in shaping the running of Caux which urgently needed to move beyond the improvisations of the first eighteen months.

It was a hard decision to make. Just before Hilary was born we had used half Stella's entire patrimony to buy a Victorian house in Putney (and no one today would believe how little we paid for it) with six bedrooms and a modest walled garden. We had just got it into shape, our daughter's first Christmas was coming up, the house already had six or eight people living in it besides ourselves, and we were dearly looking forward to bringing up our family there. We had had the thought when we bought it, however, that others in our fellowship would use it besides ourselves, but never dreamed how literally it would be fulfilled.

In that post-war setting, the call of guidance was clear: accept and go. It seemed a natural choice, hard as it might be. Countless people had made harder decisions in the war years.

We invited our close friends Peter and Monica Phelps and their children to take over the house, and moved first to Zurich in January, 1948. We finally came back to England in 1952, though we spent another year in Switzerland a little later, but we did not manage to return to our home till 28 years after we left it. It was abundantly used by all manner of friends, and by my parents in the last years of their lives. It now belongs to Hilary, who continues to use and enjoy it with like-minded friends.

So Switzerland became our second homeland, and

our admiration for the courage and tenacity of our Swiss colleagues knew, and knows, no bounds. Our son David was born in Bern at New Year 1949, on his mother's birthday. We usually lived in Caux from March to October, with winters in different Swiss cities. Our children had little chance to grow up insular, and thrived on all the varied people they knew and loved from so many countries from their tenderest years, and not least three successive Danish girls of rare quality who helped us with them through those years. Friendships they formed then are vivid now, however widely they and their friends may be scattered round the globe.

There were days in Caux in those post-war years so resonant with the mighty works of God that everything seemed possible, and nothing too hard. I wish I could convey the wonder of it. We were young, and the future was limitless.

We had yet to guage, perhaps, how much more would be needed to shift the world Godwards. But unprecedented events took place there. Faith and hope were in the ascendant, and rightly so, a spur to action however hard it might yet prove to implement these experiences on a large enough scale. But enough was achieved in those years to lead the Prime Minister of France, Robert Schuman, to call it, in his foreword to the French edition of Frank Buchman's speeches, "the beginning of a far-reaching transformation of society."

There were so many grounds for rejoicing at developments in which our work played a part, and which we lived through at first hand: the new understanding growing between France and Germany; the alternative to communism demonstrated in the industries of Northern Italy, Northern France, the Netherlands and the Ruhr; the labour-management agreements in the French textile industry, which held good for many years; the stabilising of the world price of jute, with its effect in Asia; the new relations between Holland and Germany, between Japan and former enemies – the Philippines, Korea, Australia, Malaysia, the United States; the ending of the bloodshed over the independence of Cyprus; the peaceful rather than bloody transfer to independence of more than one African country; so many events in countries great and small around the globe in which a change in people proved decisive at the critical moment, and often led to fresh initiatives in situations of potential conflict.[1]

Some people tried to belittle or undermine what we were doing – it ran counter to their whole view of life. Moscow radio, in a series of broadcasts, attacked Moral Re-Armament for "supplanting the inevitable class war by the eternal struggle between good and evil. It works for the rebuilding of the world by means of a transformation of the personality." Today, nearly forty years later, it is men in Moscow who are calling for Moral Re-Armament as the need of their troubled country.

They were years of immensely hard work at Caux. These "world assemblies" were not conferences where you fix speakers months in advance and then

---

1. See Peter Howard, *The World Rebuilt*, London, 1951.

sit listening and criticising them. They were aimed at giving people new attitudes, aims, values, freeing them from old prejudices and preconceived ideas, and enlisting them to bring a new factor into world affairs. Therefore everything had to be planned every day, and at intervals through the day, according to who was there – what themes for meetings and what speakers, what plays in the theatre, what smaller seminars needed to take place, who the guests should meet over meals. It called for a high level of teamwork.

In the midst of all this we were enjoying and bringing up our family, to which David had now been added. In the summers we lived either in a quiet corner of Caux or in nearby chalets found by our Swiss friends, and between assemblies we lived in different Swiss cities. We ourselves were often in and out of the other countries of Europe, as well as in different parts of Switzerland.

I was also up to the ears in printing and publishing in many languages – books, pamphlets, information services, reports and the rest. I immensely enjoyed book design and design for printing generally. It was always absorbing, always a challenge which raised my spirits. I used to feel that designing a piece of print was like writing a sonnet: you had to make your statement and achieve your effect within exactly defined limitations – in this case your type area, choice of type-face, length of line, and the fact that metal has hard edges and imposes its own precise limits. (This perhaps is rather less true today with the increase in litho printing, but it was a good discipline.)

I often sat through long nights working peacefully when there was urgent design work to be done, and then seeing it through the printers – who all became firm friends of ours. At the start of one summer Assembly in Caux there was an unusually large and complex amount of printing to be designed and then carried through by our printers, who were fifty minutes away down the mountain and along the lake in Lausanne. They worked a night shift as well as by day, and that year I only got to bed nine times in the first fortnight. But I enjoyed every minute.

I was never more than a hard-working amateur, but I learned a great deal from the Swiss printers and typographers with whom I worked in those years. The accolade for me came when we were living in Bern one winter. Stella was talking to Max Caflisch, one of the finest of the Swiss typographers, and he said to her, "Yesterday was a great day for me, Mrs. Belden. In the morning I had Stanley Morrison" (the great British typographer) "in my office. And then, in the afternoon – Mr Belden came!" Stella was much impressed.

Our return to England in 1952 faced us with another crisis of decision. We had looked forward so much to being in our own home together, but when I reached London in advance to make the arrangements, I found there was an urgent need for a couple to take on one of the five large houses which were then part of our headquarters. We were the only couple available at that moment, and our colleagues in London hoped very much that we would accept.

In the end we both felt it right to take on 40 Charles Street. The house, built in the late eighteenth century – Fanny Burney describes visiting it in 1782, in her diary – was really two houses, the main house in front and the old converted coach house at the back, joined by a vast basement. My old friend from Oxford days, Paul Petrocokino, who had inherited the family business his Greek grandfather had started nearly a hundred years before, had bought a twenty-seven year lease on the house for £4,700 – it hardly sounds credible today – but just after the war nobody wanted such places. It made a welcome addition to our London headquarters. The house slept twenty-two people, and such a number can live together infinitely more economically than they could in separate establishments, and there were no fares to get to work. I may add that there were eighty-six stairs from the kitchen to the childrens' bedrooms – and no lift! Stairs have never worried us since. It was a beautiful home, even if its size was daunting, and made possible seventeen fruitful years, especially when we were engaged in large-scale entertaining in connection with the Westminster Theatre.

When we arrived however a considerable amount of the furniture, beds included, had gone with Paul and Madeleine to their new home at Astonbury, in Hertfordshire. Only the carpet was left in the beautiful, Georgian-green panelled drawing room, for instance. Gradually we assembled needed furniture and pictures, some from our Putney home, some from gifts or loans from friends. I had been saving my gratuity on demobilisation to buy Stella a new coat, but we spent it instead on coverings for sofas and chairs. In the end the whole place looked splendid. Living in it was always a matter of faith, sometimes of heartfelt prayer round the breakfast table, but we had so much to be grateful for.

Though it was a tough decision to take it on, we came to love the house, and we had some wonderful occasions there over the years. And our children, though they missed some of the joys of a smaller home, grew up up in a larger world with wider sympathies and understanding.

Caux began in 1946 among the ruins of a shattered continent, and the setting of our work world-wide was daunting in its magnitude and in the depths of the fears and hatreds, sometimes centuries old, which beset the human race, quite apart from the pressing issues of poverty and hunger and injustice.

In the summer of 1986 Stella and I took part in the 40th Anniversary Assembly at Caux. The opening week was led by the French and Germans together, something which would have seemed unthinkable in 1946. There were sessions for the Americas, with strong representation from the most critical points of Central and South America alongside the North Americans. African and Asian countries were represented in strength for a "dialogue of the continents". Senior labour and management figures met from around the world, especially from Europe and Japan. The place was thronged as the sessions succeeded each other, 2,840 people altogether from sixty-three countries.

Cardinal König of Vienna, in his "Retrospect and Prospect" of the forty years of Caux, said, "For me it is an occasion to express heart-felt gratitude for all that has happened here, and in the midst of this heritage to look to the future with full confidence."

Then in 1990 we were there again as the countries of Eastern Europe streamed into Caux – Poles, Czechs, East Germans, Hungarians, Romanians, Russians, Estonians and so many more, meeting freely with the rest of the world for the first time, as they sought the moral and spiritual values which alone can guarantee their future.

Now, as in those earlier years, we are still pilgrims of the impossible, but filled with hope as well, because the impossible has been visibly happening around us all the time. That is the inevitable by-product of faith. "And Jesus looking upon them said, 'With men it is impossible but not with God: for with God all things are possible'."

9
The Creative decade

> Halts by me that footfall:
> Is my gloom after all,
> Shade of His hand . . . ?
> *Francis Thompson*

On my fortieth birthday in 1952, I had the thought in my morning quiet time, "For you, this will be the creative decade."

I was filled with pleasurable anticipation. What would it mean? Was I going to write a book? Or a play? Was I going to undertake some outstanding piece of work somewhere? I could only wait and see.

As it turned out, the next ten years were amongst the worst in my life. Difficulties of all kinds seemed to pile up, things I was engaged in seemed inadequate and, worst of all, I felt more and more dissatisfied with my own performance and the relevance of my own life. Although I did some useful work on both sides of the Atlantic, it was often heavy going, and the stresses which arose as time went on, and the unhappiness which stemmed from them, weighed on me more and more. So much so, in fact, that for the first time in nearly thirty years I began to doubt my calling and to wonder whether I was really fitted to continue in the work to which I was committed.

It was partly growing pains in our rapidly expanding work, partly personality clashes, partly the fallout of being in my forties, the age when everyone tends to feel that so many of the things they had hoped to do in life may no longer be possible, and when our energies, which could always be mobilised in an emergency, are beginning to flag a little. My own motives, good and bad, were being sifted out again. How could I or anyone be adequate for the crying needs of our age, and for all God wanted done in the world? I tried ever harder to make more farreaching decisions to do better, care more, work harder, live more unselfishly – whatever it might be that appeared to be needed – but somehow my best efforts seemed to have in them a worm of self-regard which in the end, I felt, brought them to nothing.

It was a period, too, when Frank Buchman, now in his eighties, was obviously conscious that the end of his life was drawing steadily nearer. He was making his last strenuous efforts, perhaps too strenuous, to get his team in shape for the future, to seek out the weaknesses and equip everyone with a deep enough experience for all that lay ahead. This perhaps led to more self-questioning and questioning of each other than was fully helpful. It lacked some of the resilient positive that had always been so characteristic of Frank's life. Increasingly I began to wonder whether the work would not get on better without me. And yet it had been my life for the past twenty-seven years, and still was.

There were other factors as well. Our life seemed nonstop and all demanding. I once said despondently to a couple of friends, "I've been married fourteen years and I've never had a summer holiday with my children."

As the decade drew on, in the summer of 1960, I was at crisis point. Stella and I and a few others were holding the fort in London, always a demanding time, while Frank Buchman and most of our colleagues were in Caux running the long summer World Assembly. My state of mind came to Frank's ears. A returning friend immediately brought me a message from him: "Tell Ken to take his family away for a month's holiday", with the added suggestion that we might be able to go and stay with an old friend, Elizabeth Johnstone, at her home in Cornwall.

I did not take the message seriously. It was generous of Frank to think of it, but when Caux was on and you were part of the small holding force in London, you did not reckon to go on holiday – there was far too much to do – though we would get the children away somewhere enjoyable and would slip down to join them when we could. Nor did I feel we could reasonably wish four of ourselves onto a friend just like that!

Ten days later a returning traveller brought another message from Buchman: "Has Ken gone on that holiday yet?" It sounded as if he meant it.

That evening Stella and I had to go to a reception. We arrived early, and as we walked into the room there was only one other person there – Elizabeth Johnstone, on one of her rare visits to London. She came over to us at once, all smiles, and said, "I'm so glad to see you both. I wonder if you can help me.

My mother is abroad for the summer and I'm alone in the house with two Italian maids. Do you know any family among our friends who would like to come down for a month? They wouldn't have a thing to do."

When we had recovered our composure we asked, "Would you mind if it was us?"

It was, of course, the best summer holiday we had ever had with our children, then thirteen and eleven. A different cove to swim in every time they wanted to, the moors, picnics, the Minack Theatre, the fishing villages, and the spacious grounds of Elizabeth's home, and ample time for everything.

At the same time I was still racked by uncertainty about my future, which would affect us all. I spent long hours by myself in a deck chair in the rose garden trying to figure out life afresh, and praying for some light on it all. It was marvellously relaxing and refreshing, but in all that month I came away with only two clear convictions, and perhaps they were enough.

The first was: The battle in the world exists. The battle between good and evil, faith and materialism. You cannot evade the fact that the world is a battle ground.

The second conviction was: You can choose to fight or not to fight. You can be in the battle or stay out of it. It's entirely up to you.

On balance I was sure I would rather fight the battle, however ineptly than not be in it at all. I decided to stick around and, on our return to

London, to do what came to hand and see where it led me.

So thanks to Frank Buchman's discerning care I stayed, but it would be idle to say that I saw much more daylight, though I was inwardly more at peace. The autumn went by, and Christmas, and a few days later I found myself in Caux for the New Year Assembly. I was usually in Caux at this time, because immediately after the conference we always had a meeting of the Council of the Swiss Foundation responsible for Caux, of which I was a member for many years. This year was also one of the rare times (and as it turned out, the last) when Frank Buchman himself was there over Christmas and New Year.

My own way forward seemed as opaque as ever. I seemed to be holding on more by stubbornness than anything else. At midnight on New Year's eve I found myself alone in the coffee lounge in Mountain House, feeling in deep despair. If even my firmest decisions got me nowhere, what could I do? If I couldn't even make the needed right decision for my life, how could I ever go forward?

As I pondered this in the silent building, I realised, "There is nothing more you can do. Nothing more you can decide. You don't know what to ask for. This is the end of that road."

Then as I thought on, "There is only one course open to you: throw yourself on the mercy of Christ, and see what He can do for you."

So I tried to do this, and went off to bed.

Next morning, when my alarm went off at half-past five, I woke – and realised that I felt completely different. The light had come on again. It was like that January morning in Oxford, so long ago. I did not know what had happened but I knew the block in my own spirit had shifted.

When I began my quiet time I had a curious thought: Read the passages in the Old Testament about clay and potters. I looked them up in the concordance at the back of my Bible and worked my way through them. There are quite a few, but one leapt out of the page and shouted at me: "Does the clay say to the Potter, What are you making out of me?"

In that moment I saw it all. My mind and spirit clarified. For years I had been badgering the Potter to shape me in ways that I, or other people, thought best, or most desirable or, indeed, most useful for our calling. But all that was over. From now on the Potter could make of my lump of clay whatever He wanted to, unimpeded by advice from me. It was no longer any business of mine – it never had been. From now on I would never again worry about whether I was doing well or doing badly, going up or going down, moving forward or at a standstill. Never again would I worry what anyone else thought of me or how I stood in their estimation. If I fell into sin, my friends would undoubtedly tell me. Otherwise I would just get on with the next thing I was shown to do, and let my Heavenly Father make of my life whatever he had in mind. I ended that quiet time a free man again.

So different did I feel that I wrote Frank Buchman a note telling him about it and dropped it in to his room on the way to breakfast. A couple of days later I was sitting near him in a small planning meeting, and when I contributed something he suddenly turned to me and said with great warmth and emphasis, "Why, Ken, you're changed!"

"Well, Frank," I replied, "I'm glad to have it on such good authority!"

I only saw him to talk with him once again. In June that year I came out to Caux for his 83rd birthday, bringing with me the first copy of a new pocket edition of his collected speeches which I had re-edited and re-designed, and seen through the presses. I sat and talked with him alone in his sitting rom as I gave him the first copy. "The tide is rising in Britain, but it must rise much faster yet", were his last words to me as I left. Six weeks later he died.

Six months later I was asked to become a trustee of the Westminster Memorial Trust, which owned and ran the Westminster Theatre, and almost immediately afterwards was made Chairman of the Trust, which I remained for the next eighteen years.[1] We were just beginning many years of continuous showings of our own plays, in great variety, eight shows a week throughout the year, with professional actors and actresses. These showings were backed by a continuous campaign up and down Britain and across the continent to bring in the audiences, especially from the industrial areas and other fields of national need with many far-reaching results in people's lives and situations.

1. See Chapter 10.

In the next ten years we also carried through a building programme which more than doubled the size of our buildings on land we already owned beside the theatre. We had to raise over half a million pounds for the first phase, and a quarter of a million for the second, when we took the top off the theatre and created a new administrative centre for Moral Re-Armament up there.

In the same decade I did write a book and numerous pamphlets as well, and was constantly travelling and speaking up and down this country and on the continent. I went to India to bring back Rajmohan Gandhi's superb musical, *India Arise*, and on the way back went to Khartoum to receive the gift of leather from the Sudan government which they had offered for our new building.

During these ten years over a million people from more than a hundred countries put down their money at our box office to see our plays. A number of the plays were filmed, and some were produced in other languages and in other countries, as far away as Japan and New Zealand. The theatre proved a bastion of God's truth in a period when the kitchen sink, the theatre of cruelty and the theatre of the absurd dominated the London scene. We had a nationwide conference at the theatre every weekend for fourteen years, many of which I led myself, and which fuelled a sustained advance throughout the land.

So which was the creative decade?

In my view, still the first: not because I did anything creative in it but because in the end I stepped out of the picture and let God Almighty do something creative in me. It was highly uncomfortable, very necessary, long overdue and, in the end, creative in the following years in wholly unforeseen ways.

10
"Fountains of felicity"

TOM SHILLINGTON was killed when he went to help the wounded driver of his tank in a battle in the Western Desert. Hugh Beresford, second in command to Lord Louis Mountbatten in HMS Kelly, was lost when the ship was sunk off Crete. Hugh Kitson was killed training the New Zealand Air Force. Michael Sitwell died when his landing craft was lost in the Channel in the invasion of Normandy. Roger Faure, Paris architect, was killed commanding his battery in the defence of Calais. Cecil Pugh, RAF chaplain, gave his life when he insisted on staying with the wounded men who could not be saved from their sinking troopship, and won a posthumous George Cross. Frederic Ramm, the Norwegian editor-resistance leader, died through imprisonment in Germany. . . . The list goes on for many pages, men and women in Moral Re-Armament from every part of the world and many nationalities: they fought and died in the Allied Forces or in the concentration camps and resistance movements.

All the ones I have named, and many, many more I knew, and some were close friends. It was in their honour, and to help fulfil the aims for which they died, that twenty British couples who had lost fathers, brothers, husbands, sons or friends in the war set up a fund in 1946 for a unique memorial.

Their conviction was to buy a West End theatre which could be a living memorial for generations to come, by mounting plays which would proclaim the truths most needed in the coming years.

When they located the Westminster Theatre, an intimate theatre seating 600 people, the money was raised through 2,857 individuals gifts, many of them from returning servicemen who gave their gratuities. The ownership of the theatre was vested in the Westminster Memorial Trust. The theatre was commissioned for its new role on Remembrance Sunday, 1946, the stage crowded with men and women of all ranks who had served or were still serving in the Allied Forces around the world.

We opened with a historic run of Alan Thornhill's play *The Forgotten Factor*. A hundred thousand people came to see it through that long, icy winter, before its extensive tour of the British coalfields where it had a far-reaching effect. During the next fifteen years we used the theatre ourselves when we had plays that were part of our strategy in Britain, and for the rest of the time let it out to other professional companies to cover its costs and keep our admirable technical staff together.

It was during one of the periods when we were using it ourselves, in the early summer of 1955, that I happened to go down to the theatre one day and, as I looked about me, standing outside, a conviction struck me with the force of revelation. The theatre, converted from an eighteenth century chapel, stood on an irregularly shaped corner site in Palace Street. The theatre itself occupied just over half this site.

The rest included a small parking space, a nineteenth century cottage full of dry rot, a tiny garden, a small dressing room wing, and a ramshackle scenery store.

What I suddenly saw, as no one else seemed to have done before, was that if we cleared everything away, there would be beside the theatre a superb site of almost equal size, and that here was the place not only to expand our theatre facilities, which was much needed, but also to provide the future centre for our work. What was more, it was freehold and already belonged to us. Every other property we held, including our administrative centre in Hays Mews, was leasehold – and the leases were running out.

So strongly did I feel about these possibilities that I asked two young architects, Anthony Sursham and William Bell, to make some imaginative drawings showing what could be done with the site. Gordon Hassell, a senior trustee, took them out to Caux to show Frank Buchman, who was deeply interested by them.

As an idea it was ten years ahead of its time. But in 1964, at Peter Howard's suggestion, we launched a preliminary planning application. When Howard died so unexpectedly a few months later many of our colleagues felt strongly that the building should be raised in his memory, and in June 1965 the plan was launched at a crowded meeting of 700 people from all over the country in the theatre.[1] In November 1966 the new building was opened by Shri Rajmohan Gandhi, a close colleague of Howard's, and dedicated

1. See *The Story of the Westminster Theatre*, London, 1965

by the Bishop of Colchester. By the following June, two years after the launching, everything was paid for.

Some years before this, as I mentioned earlier, I had become involved in the Westminster Theatre in a wholly unforeseen way. Early in 1962 some of the original trustees, now in their eighties, felt they should retire. They wanted to appoint some younger men. Bunny Austin, whose wife Phyllis Konstam played a central part in the development of our theatre, was an immediate choice. So was John Vickers, chairman of a Yorkshire oil business, who followed his father Farrar Vickers onto the trust. But then came a request from the trustees for one member of the Council of the Oxford Group to become a trustee to link the two bodies more closely.

Through fortune, fate or Providence there were only two of these creatures in the country at the time – Roland Wilson, the Secretary of the Oxford Group and myself. All the rest were serving overseas. Roly said to me, "I don't see how I can carry being Secretary and be an adequate trustee as well, so it had better be you."

This is the way so many of the momentous moves in life seem to be made. We agonise for weeks over some minor domestic arrangement, but the decisions that affect our whole lives often seem to be settled walking down a corridor.

I found myself both appalled and exhilarated at the prospect. Appalled because my life seemed over full already, and exhilarated because I felt there were great developments ahead for the theatre, and my spirits rose at the prospect of having a hand in shaping them.

So I became a trustee in February, 1962 and a few weeks later the rest of the trustees combined to inform me that I was now Chairman of the Trust and would naturally be their spokesman in future. It was not till eighteen years later that I was able to bow myself out. I had a lot to learn, and fast.

It was in the Spring of 1964 that Peter Howard said to me one day, "I think the time has come to launch the building programme at the theatre." We had talked about the possibilities more than once in the previous years. Now we consulted widely among our friends, and they all agreed that the time had come to move on it.

By now we were running our own plays all through the year and it was painfully obvious that the theatre by itself was inadequate for our purposes. Two minutes after the curtain fell at the end of the play, everyone was out on the street, and this was just the moment when people wanted to sit down and talk about the implications of the play for their lives. Palace Street on a winter's night was hardly the place. We needed a restaurant, and a spacious foyer in place of the cramped pocket handkerchief-sized entrance we had. Our dressing rooms were quite inadequate in our view, and some of them were in the cellars, the crypt of the old chapel. We had been praised in a broadcast by the Secretary of Equity as a shining example of a theatre which had tried to improve its old accommodation for the actors, but we ourselves felt they deserved something much better. Many other improvements were needed including facilities for providing meals for our frequent conferences, to say nothing of office space which was very limited.

We were put in touch with Sir Hugh Casson, and he and his partner saw through the preliminary planning application. But before we had gone further, and just after Peter Howard had suddenly died of a lethal virus in Latin America, I had a phone call from Hugh Casson: would I come to lunch with him? There he had to tell me with great regret that they could not go ahead with the theatre plan for us, much as they wanted to. The reason was that under the Robbins report the university in Birmingham was to be greatly enlarged and as they were the official architects to the university, this meant that their resources would be stretched to the limit for the coming years. They were more than disappointed. They would find a worthy substitute and would speedily suggest two possibilities and leave us to choose.

When John Reid came to see us we realised we need look no further. He and his equally qualified wife and partner, Sylvia, were a delight to work with. He is not only highly imaginative and skilled as an architect, but is also an industrial designer and a lighting expert (he designed the lighting for Coventry Cathedral). We could not have been in better hands. When John Reid saw the Trustees' brief at our first meeting (he later said it was the best brief he had ever received) listing what we wanted, he said, "All you need is a site four times the size and a building eight stories high!" But he and Sylvia worked out how to do it, and when the building was opened the journal *The Designer* called their achievement "a miracle of imaginative exploitation of precious space."

There remained, however, the question of how to find the money. There was enthusiastic support up and down the land, but it was going to cost at least half-a-million pounds, real money in those days – I suppose it would be more like three or four million today. I had imagined that if we really found ourselves stuck we could always get a bridging loan to tide us over. But this was now the period of Harold Wilson's credit freeze when you could hardly borrow the price of a bus ticket from the banks. It was all going to have to be raised by volunteers, and quickly.

For the next two years this was a matter for daily, and sometimes hourly, prayer by all of us concerned, both individually and by a group which met every day. I spent many hours trying to search the Mind of the Almighty on how to proceed, and we all learned to move in the conviction that it was not in our capacities but in what God Himself would do that the answer lay.

If you know yours is the signature that has to go at the foot of a contract for half-a-million pounds (it turned out to be a good deal more before we finished) "it wonderfully concentrates the mind" as Dr. Johnson would say. I spent many hours thinking it out to satisfy myself that, under God, it was possible to envisage raising what was needed. One great help at the start was the promise of substantial help from another charitable trust. It did not all come at once, but in the end it added up to £200,000 which was a massive help. Nothing else came remotely near it. A friend introduced me to a director of one of the big five banks and I consulted him about it. He was a man of faith and said to me, "You have this large promise, and if you believe your rate of fund raising can keep pace with your building costs, then I would advise you to go ahead", which was encouraging.

Then a friend of mine in the motor trade said to me, "It's quite simple really: if you need to raise, say, £50,000, you just get fifty people to give a thousand pounds each". The only difficulty was, I didn't know fifty people who could give a thousand each, or anything like it. But then it struck me that people are very resourceful, and many perhaps who couldn't give a thousand pounds might raise a thousand, given time to do it. To satisfy myself that it was something that could be done, before I raised it publicly, I sat down and made a list of a hundred people I knew, or small groups who naturally worked together, who I thought might be able to do such a thing if they felt moved to. Then at the launching of the whole project at the Westminster in June, 1965, I asked whether a hundred individuals or groups would each pledge themselves to raise £1,000 by Christmas. In the end, 118 fulfilled this pledge, and most of the names were on my original list, had they known it. Some efforts were spectacular, like the three senior ladies in Edinburgh, all retired missionaries with hardly a penny between them, though a lot of faith, all in or near their eighties, who not only raised

£1,000 together, rounding it off with gifts at the eightieth birthday party of one of them, but went on to raise another £500 the following year. Don't ask me how they did it. I haven't the faintest idea.

And then the gifts began to come in from other countries. The Netherlands headed the list for generosity, followed hard by Sweden. In all, people in fifty-one countries made gifts in cash or kind. In the Sudan, one of Howard's devoted friends was a member of the cabinet, Sayed Buth Diu, President of the Liberal Party, an enormous, warm-hearted southerner. On his initiative the Sudan government offered us all the leather we needed. What do you do with leather in such a building? BOAC flew a specimen hide from the government tannery in Khartoum. John Reid decided to panel the foyer with it, and also used it on the doors into the auditorium and other places. It looks superb. He insisted on keeping all the original scratches and bumps and Arabic numerals stamped on the backs of the cattle. "That shows it's really leather," he said to me. "If you refine it too much it just looks like PVC!"

This is not the moment to review all that went into that period, the hazards and the excitements. As the months went by I learned a great deal about faith. At one point I had to go for three weeks to India, to Kenya, to Ethiopia briefly, and to Khartoum for the official presentation of the leather. When I got back I found that for reasons wholly out of anyone's control the cost of the building had gone up by £60,000 (it turned out to be nearer £100,000 in the end).

I felt in considerable anguish. Up till then things

seemed to be going along well, and I thought our pace of fund raising would just keep pace with the bills. Now everything was in jeopardy. Where could we turn to bridge such a chasm? To meet the crisis I spent a week writing to friends around the world and up and down the British Isles, telling them what had happened and asking them to pray for the increased needs to be provided. My secretary-colleague, Heather Hopcraft, typed a mile and a quarter of tape that week. From that moment the gifts never ceased coming in till the building was completely paid for the following summer.

It was at this time that I read a verse of Thomas Traherne's which contained the line that altered my whole attitude to such difficulties and the way I thought about them:

"Wants are the fountains of felicitie."

It had never occurred to me that needs could be the fountains of happiness and well-being. I had always regarded it as a great trial to feel in need, whether financially or in my own spiritual life. It felt much happier when everything was going smoothly and under control. But that, I now realised, was trusting in myself, not in God. It was when I felt in dire need as I was at this moment, faced with massive difficulties, that I could see the power and the generosity of God in action, and rejoice.

Time and again in those months I would get on my knees and say, "Lord, this is quite beyond me. But this building is your idea, so please show what You can do in this present predicament."

There was a period leading up to the opening and afterwards when we needed to raise a thousand pounds a day for weeks on end to keep pace with our bills, which were coming in from all quarters as the work was completed. We all prayed fervently and daily, and the money came in steadily. People were amazing. I had to go out to Caux briefly at one point, for a meeting of the Swiss Foundation. There, sitting in the main hall as I walked in, was one of the great ladies of the Netherlands, Lottie van Beuningen, decorated by her Queen for heroically saving the lives of hundreds of her fellow countrymen during the wartime occupation, widow of the head of the Dutch coal board, and now in her eighties. She called me over to her. "I've got something here for the new building," she said. "It's all I was allowed to bring out with me." She fished a banknote out of her capacious handbag and gave it to me. It was for 5,000 guilders, and burned a hole in my pocket all the way back to London till I could put it safely into the hands of Nigel Morshead, my fellow trustee who had given up his position in the City to be Treasurer of the building fund.

On another occasion we were in Cardiff. The new building was to be clad entirely in beautiful, riven Welsh slate, forty-two tons of it. It was half the cost of Portland stone and keeps its looks indefinitely. People in Wales had pledged themselves to raise the cost. Cardiff was the first of two meetings to launch their fund. The other was nearer the slate quarries, at Carnarvon. Suddenly in the Cardiff meeting a little, wizened, bent old miner slowly made his way through the crowded hall to the platform. It was Tom Evans, in the pits for a lifetime and also a former Glamorgan county councillor, who loved the Westminster. When he stepped onto the platform he turned to the audience and said, "I don't want to make a speech. I just want to give a week of my pension." He handed me the unopened envelope and went down to his place again. It was a moving moment, and typical of how it was all done, not from surplus but from sacrifice.

It was a marking day in November, 1966 when Shri Rajmohan Gandhi opened the new building and unveiled the memorial plaque to Peter Howard, superbly carved on a tall panel of the Welsh slate. It carried the words his old friend Lord Hailsham had used at his memorial service in St. Martin-in-the-fields: "He was determined that goodness should not perish from the earth, that light should conquer darkness."[1] An opposite plaque commemorating the gift of the Welsh slate that clads the building was unveiled by Lloyd George's grand-daughter, Margaret Barrett, while a Welsh miners' choir sang the Welsh national anthem.

Then, in a theatre crowded in every corner, the new building was dedicated by the Rt. Rev. Roderick Coote, Bishop of Colchester. It was indeed a day to

1. The seven foot high panel was designed by William Gardner, a foremost designer in this field. He said to me, "From what you tell me, Peter Howard was a man of burning integrity, so I have surmounted the inscription with the symbol of the burning sun." It was carved by Kevin Cribb, a former pupil of Eric Gill.

remember. After Rajmohan Gandhi's address four of Peter Howard's grandchildren presented him with one of their grandfather's favourite books. Mrs. Peter Howard spoke, with her daughter and son-in-law, Anne and Patrick Wolridge-Gordon. We heard from the architect John Reid and others, and then went on in the evening to the inaugural dinner in the new dining room, for 172 guests, where Prince Richard of Hesse was guest of honour. Afterwards we all went down to the theatre to see the new musical, *It's our country, Jack*. What a day.

"Wants are the fountains of felicity." It applies in so many places besides financial need. In those days I often had to lie in bed when the alarm went off and pray for courage before I could even sit up for my morning quiet time! But it is always at the point of need that we find Christ. St. Peter couldn't walk on the water till he got out of the boat, with Christ to sustain his faith – and rescue him when his faith faltered and he started to sink.

One of our many debts to St. Paul is his emphasis, again and again, on the generosity of God. He is a friend of royal generosity, "that glorious generosity of His . . . that free and generous grace which has overflowed into our lives." It is that generosity we are meant to live in for all our many needs: we can bring them to Him in total confidence that He will fill us to overflowing from "the fountains of felicity".

In 1946, for legal reasons valid at the time, the Westminster Theatre had been vested not in the Oxford Group itself but in a separate body, the Westminster Memorial Trust. Thirty years later these reasons no longer applied, and my last action as Chairman of the Trust, with my fellow trustees and the approval of the Charity Commissioners, was to transfer the entire building to the Oxford Group, who then assumed responsibility for it from 1 August, 1980. Our lawyers told us at the time that it was the largest gift from one charity to another in this century.

In 1991, owing in part to rising costs of production, the Council of the Oxford Group decided that the time had come to part with the theatre and seek new headquarters elsewhere. What the outcome of this decision will be remains to be seen.

11
Remakers of the world?

> Christ cared more for humanity than for religion. What Christ came here for was to make a better world . . . a prodigious task, to recreate the world.
>
> *Henry Drummond*

> We must remake the world. The task is nothing less than that.
>
> *Frank Buchman*

FRANK BUCHMAN came up to me one day outside Lady Margaret Hall, one of the centres of the Oxford Group conference in Oxford that year, 1936. "Ken", he said, "how do you think we ought to describe the meaning of our work? Should it be rebuilding the world, remaking the world, reconstructing the world? What would you say? I'm inclined to think remaking the world is the right way to put it."

He had used the words for the first time a few weeks before in a speech in New England, but he was still searching in his spirit and was testing reactions among his friends. It was part of his ceaseless quest to raise the expectations of men and women of faith about their task.

Remaking the world it became, and if there is one

lesson more than another that distinguished what we learned from him, it is to have a world outlook and a world setting for what we do, however locally we may be tied. How easily the universal Church becomes parochial. How much more easily we ordinary citizens become absorbed in our own affairs. But to Frank your commitment to God was inadequate unless it became a world commitment, even if the only way you could ever travel was through your imagination in your prayers and thought for people. "God so loved the *world*. . . ."

I have sometimes heard people react against the thought of remaking the world, calling it unrealistic, impossible, presumptuous even, though we are clearly called to take part in bringing the Kingdom of God on earth. Even less convincingly, some people say, "You've been at it for fifty years and you haven't done it yet, so why go on talking about it?" Fifty years? It's taken more than fifty years to agree to dig a hole under the Channel. What do people imagine remaking the world entails? A big effort for ten years and then we can all go home?

I am sure Frank Buchman never thought of it in these terms. His battle was always with people who want to live and think too small. He did not see remaking the world as some task to be finished by a fixed date in the foreseeable future. To him it was a process which goes on to the end of time. But to have as your aim the remaking of the world as Christ would have it is to put everything you do, every person you meet into a new perspective. It may show you responsibilities in society it never occurred to you to take up before: in your trade union, your borough council, your university; over the environment, at home or overseas; in care for disadvantaged people in this country or in the Third World. The possibilities are endless and the most unexpected people move out to take them on. "Ordinary people start doing the extraordinary thing when they are guided by God."

My friend Stanley Barnes, at the time he met the Oxford Group in the 'thirties, was a rising young manager in the milk business in the Cotswolds. Then the government of Malta put out a request for someone to reorganise the milk production of the island, which badly needed it. Barnes offered to volunteer. His friends in the business tried to dissuade him: it would be a dead end, among all those goats, and he had a prosperous future assured where he was. But his inner conviction was to go, so he went, and did an outstanding job. He was still at it when war broke out, and spent part of the war years there organising the distribution of petrol to the RAF instead. But after the war, his experience in Malta took him to Pakistan and Indonesia for many years, as well as to India and other countries, and he became a world authority on milk supply in the Third World. He has written some compelling books about it.[1] From his base in Australia he has become the adviser to governments. All because one young man decided to follow

---

1. Books by Stanley Barnes include *Two Hundred Million Hungry Children*, and, most recently, *Children in Crisis*, both published in Australia.

the guidance of God and obeyed, even though it seemed to cut across his "career prospects". It has been his part in remaking the world.

We face such vast and daunting problems in the world today, but to meet them we need, most of all, the men and women who know that God can free them, guide them, remake them. People who know this for themselves can tackle any situation that becomes their concern. Drummond, so far ahead of his time in these matters, writes of the crucial need for "good men": "By far the greatest thing a man can do for his city is to be a good man. Simply to live there as a good man . . . is the first and highest contribution anyone can make . . . Such good men will not merely content themselves with being good men. They will be forces – according to their measure, public forces. Of set purpose, they will serve." And good women too!

Nowadays, as so many thousands of volunteers in famine relief and many other areas of need have shown, to be such a force and to serve can take you to the ends of the earth. It is a new element in the world's life.

In the turmoil of our world, so much of it a legacy from our Western domination, it is also plain that we have to learn to operate at a much deeper level than most of the political and economic efforts to meet the situations.

However, more people have an instinct for what is really needed than we sometimes realise. In 1948, Stella and I flew from Los Angeles to Washington with a group of men and women who were playing varied roles in the reconstruction of Europe, for a lunch with General Marshall. Marshall was then Secretary of State and in the throes of piloting the Marshall Plan, crucial for post-war Europe, through Congress.

We sat down about forty, perhaps, with Marshall and with Paul Hoffman, his administrator for the Marshall Plan. These were men and women from all the main European countries. They included Austria and Germany – men who had opposed Hitler all the way and were now Ministers President, Ministers, Members or Speakers of some of the German regional parliaments, leaders of trade unions, industrialists, the man who was to be the first post-war ambassador from Germany to Britain, and so on. The French, the Italians, the Dutch and Scandinavians were there, as well as the British. They had all been taking part in the tenth anniversary assembly of Moral Re-Armament in California.

Marshall was keen to know what these men really felt. How were they going to respond to Marshall Aid? Would they use it wisely or was it money down the drain for America? How did they view the future of the continent from inside its borders?

When a number of the men spoke on behalf of the rest, including two veteran socialist leaders from Bavaria, the effect was extraordinary. Man after man said, in different ways, from different countries, but with the same unmistakeable message, "We are grateful beyond words for American aid and for all you are planning to do to help us – it means life or death for our people. But we would like to tell you that there is something we need even more than material aid if we are to rebuild Europe: we need aid in the moral and spiritual reconstruction of our countries. This is what is needed above everything else, and only this will make material aid fully effective."

Marshall was visibly moved. He had not foreseen that these men, in such dire situations, would feel like this and would say so, so forthrightly. It encouraged him at a key moment in seeing through the Marshall aid programme.

It also illustrates the fact that there is more to putting countries and continents on the right course than economic and political measures alone can achieve, vital as they may be, and this was never more true than it is today after the recent events in Eastern Europe.

The role of people of faith, in addition to all they may do to improve the structures of society and render them more just and compassionate, is to supply this missing element. It is to create men and women who are free from bitterness and prejudice, who are hate-free and greed-free, who are colour-blind, with a love for everyone of every race, people who can share the experiences which can transform anyone into a constructive force. And as always it has to start with ourselves.

Immense forces are massing against faith and moral standards today, from the humanist desire to expunge them from human consciousness right through to the drugs and sex mafia making their millions out of the moral collapse that so swiftly follows losing that sense of God that we are born to hold.

To turn that tide is a world-wide task and we shall need every ally we can find. Is this a predicament, perhaps, which should lead us to rethink our attitudes to the people of other faiths? It will surely take the concerted action of all who revere God to shift humanity into a more sane direction.

What we need, it seems to me, is the unity of men and women who seek above all to find and do the will of God. There is only one God, however widely our understanding of Him differs. To us He is Father, Son and Holy Spirit. If a Jew or a Hindu or a Muslim opens his heart and mind to God, there is only One to answer him or her, as there is for us. In spite of the centuries of differing cultures and forms of thought, the truth persists: when man listens, God speaks. This is the uniting point. It does not minimise differences or say that one way is as good as another, but it does enable all men and women of faith to work together and respect each other as they seek and obey God's inner word.

To some Christians, I find the idea of moving in friendship with people of other faiths seems repugnant, but in a country like our own, where it is said there are now more Muslims than Methodists, it is high time we gave fresh thought to what our attitude should be. In one school where my daughter taught in London there were twenty-seven mother tongues, and while Easter and Whitsun and Christmas were celebrated so were Divali and Id. We live in a fast changing world and many past attitudes call for re-assessment.

At Oxford in the 'thirties, one of the women

undergraduates on our team was Charis Waddy who impressed us by becoming the first woman to read Arabic and Hebrew Studies, which she crowned by taking a First Class degree. She had spent many of her younger years in Jerusalem, and the relations of the three great faiths centred there, among whom she had many friends, had long preoccupied her. Today she is an acknowledged and sought-after authority on Islam and, a dedicated Christian, has devoted many years to building bridges of understanding between the faiths. She has been decorated for her work by the government of Pakistan, and her best-known book, *The Muslim Mind*[1] has recently been reissued in a revised edition. At its launching, the Principal of the Muslim College in London said that her book "not only built bridges but spoke to all our hearts." On the cover Dr. Waddy quotes the Arab proverb, "What comes from the lips reaches the ear. What comes from the heart reaches the heart", and perhaps this is a key to what our own attitudes should become in our own country and beyond.

Lord Runcie, when he was Archbishop of Canterbury, spoke of his visit to India and the need for true dialogue "which would overcome divisiveness and create new conditions for greater fellowship and deeper communion" between Christians and those of other traditions. "It can help us", he added, "to recognise that other faiths than our own are genuine mansions of the Spirit, with many rooms to be dis-

---

1. *The Muslim Mind*, by Dr. Charis Waddy, Grosvenor Books, London, new and revised edition, 1990.

covered, rather than solitary fortresses to be attacked."

The Second Vatican Council expressed the same thought in saying that the Church "rejects nothing which is true and holy in these religions", and sincerely respects those ways of living and acting which may differ from what she holds and teaches, "but which none the less often reflect the brightness of the truth which is the light of all men."

The Vatican II declarations adds, "We cannot call on God, the Father of all men, if there are any men whom we refuse to treat as brothers, since all men are created in God's image."[1]

It is one of the least attractive sides of human nature that we so easily detest or despise people who do not see things our way. The world is full of violent examples – people ruthlessly killed and maimed because they dissent from some other people's view of the world or some others' ideology.

Even among Christians, I almost said especially among Christians, deviations from the views, doctrines, practices of any group are often harshly regarded. For centuries Christians resolutely condemned each other to an agonising death at the stake, supposedly for the sake of their souls but actually out of revenge for not submitting to the views of the prevailing authority in power. Even today we can be very stand-offish towards others in the same congregation who see things differently from us.

So it is no wonder that our attitude to people

1. Published by the Catholic Truth Society, London, 1965.

of other faiths has often been one of contempt or condemnation, sometimes of pogrom and persecution, and always a total assurance that we are right and they are wrong.

It is not a very winning approach. We as Christians believe that God made the supreme revelation of Himself in Jesus Christ, and that in Him all the highest aspirations of every faith will find fulfilment. But if we imagine we can march out and forthwith convert everyone to this opinion we are hardly living in the real world. There is too much past history for that, too many appalling cruelties, too much ruthless exploitation and expropriation by people from lands which called themselves Christian. Our one hope is to try to live our faith so fully that people of other faiths may want to come to know Jesus Christ as He really is, not as we have misrepresented Him down the centuries, and might find the grace one day to forgive us.

Could more of us live a life which not only proclaims Christ but draws people to him? They are not always the same thing. I have noticed how often in countries like India people find Christ immensely attractive. It is Christians they can't stomach. After 300 years of exploitation and conquest by God-fearing Westerners, it is amazing they can be as polite to us as they are, or that so many do in fact find their way into the faith which is still, to them, the religious expression of the Raj they fought so hard to get rid of.

One of my best friends in India once said to me over the lunch table, "Ken, I want you to know that what means most to me is my relationship with Jesus Christ." I was profoundly surprised. But I believed him. He is a very honest and perceptive thinker, and never writes a superficial line. I was moved by what he said. He has never felt an urge, so far as I know, to become a Christian formally. That is something quite different. Am I to tell him he cannot have a relationship with Christ unless he has been baptised and received into the Church, when he so obviously already has one? Christ is unfettered by our rules, and He acts where He will throughout the world.

In London a few years ago I ran into an old friend, Sayed Ahmed el Mahdi, grandson of the great Mahdi and himself now the spiritual leader of six million Muslims in the Sudan. He was on a short visit to England. He told me that a day or two before, on Battle of Britain Sunday, he had found himself in Canterbury Cathedral during the Remembrance Day service. "There was I", he said, "in my Arab dress in the cathedral, completely transported out of myself." He spoke of Christian friends in the Sudan and said, "I believe the future peace of the world may depend on Christians and Muslims learning to understand one another."

Pope John Paul expressed a similar conviction on his visit to Turkey in 1979, when he spoke of the peoples of Islam "who hold like us the faith of Abraham and the one Almighty and merciful God", and spoke of the urgent need for Christians and Muslims "to recognise and develop the spiritual bonds that unite us", for the sake of the peace of the world.

People have sometimes misunderstood why those in Moral Re-Armament have built bonds of friendship and action with men and women of other faiths over many years. This is surely the truly Christian approach, through dialogue and mutual respect and a common search for the will of God. It is an approach which the Oxford Group has pursued for more than fifty years and which is, today, becoming the accepted attitude in the Churches. It is to fail to do this which is less than Christian. How would Christ Himself approach people of other faiths? How did He? He held up the Good Samaritan, whose religion was detested by the Jews, as an example of how to "love your neighbour as yourself"; He commended the Roman centurion for showing more faith than anyone in Israel, and the Phoenician mother for her great faith; and He told the woman at the well that it was not a question of whether you should worship God in Samaria or Jerusalem, but of worshipping Him in spirit and truth. What He seems to have responded to is the reality of love and faith wherever they were found.

For myself, I have found it a ceaseless challenge through the years to live in the reality of the battle for the world. It has meant shedding many narrow viewpoints, many preconceived ideas about where and at what I should work, much reluctance at being disturbed, much resistance to needed change in myself. But it is the dimension in which we are meant to live and the battle we are meant to fight. It is our calling: "Thy kingdom come. Thy will be done on earth, as it is in heaven."

12
"Greet the unseen with a cheer!"

> The best is yet to be,
> The last of life, for which the first was made:
> Our times are in His hand
> Who saith "A whole I planned,
> Youth shows but half; trust God: see all, nor be afraid".
>
> *Robert Browning*

GROWING old is a strange business. Peter Howard described it with moving insight in the opening soliloquy by the old man in his last play, *Happy Deathday*. Part of you moves with all the mental vigour and imagination you have always known, mellowed and matured, you hope, by experience. Part of you moves at a different tempo altogether as physical energies can no longer keep pace. Sometimes you become impatient with yourself and other people.

When you are in your seventies and eighties you often think about dying, a subject of absorbing interest, and try to be as objective about it as you can manage. You do your best to lay hold on the promises of faith, and to trust in the world you hope will open up around you before long.

"Greet the unseen with a cheer!" was one of

father's favourite lines in Browning. It matched the irrepressible side of his nature. He loved Browning, and wrote and lectured on him. I had a line from the great verse beginning, "One who never turned his back but marched breast forward", inscribed on his memorial.

"Greet the unseen with a cheer!" certainly matched his own approach to eternal life. A day or two before he died he suddenly opened his eyes and looked at my stepmother and myself beside his bed, and said in a voice full of unexpected strength, "We know what we know, don't we? And it's wonderful."

It has never seemed to me particularly difficult to imagine the possibility of a dimension of life which is outside space and outside time; a dimension which is intangible, invisible and unknowable by our human sense equipment; a dimension which, for all we can tell, lies all around us without our knowing it. It is impossible for us to conceive what such a dimension is like – it is too remote from anything in our experience. But the possibility of its existence is not hard to imagine.

Every day of our lives, as it is, we are surrounded and our bodies penetrated by a world of sight and sound and colour which we cannot see, cannot feel, cannot hear, of which we are totally unaware and to whose existence we could have no clue without our radio and television equipment. We have come to accept such things as normal phenomena of our world. But how would you explain them to a headhunter from the New Guinea Highlands who had never heard of anything outside his mountain valley?

They would present him with an impossible leap in thought and concept.

A mouse nesting in a piano might find his furry ears inundated by the playing of a Brendel or an Ashkenazy, and would certainly be aware that something was going on. But how would you convey to his mouse-mind any conception of Beethoven? Or of music itself, and how it affects the human spirit? You would be speaking of a world not only unknown but unknowable.

These are inadequate analogies, but they illustrate the point that there is no inherent difficulty in imagining the existence of an order of reality beyond anything we can see or touch, hear or locate, analyse or measure by the normal processes of earth. Nor does it seem impossible that the human spirit can enter that dimension when the body it has been linked with in this world has to be discarded.

Three times in my life I have stood by the bedside when someone I deeply loved has died. To me, these are the moments that have spoken most strongly of eternal life. At one moment the person you have always known is there, however weak: the next, that loved person has gone. The outward appearance that is so familiar is still there, exactly the same for the moment, but the person is no longer there. And at that moment it is almost impossible not to believe that that person is still alive, but no more in a dimension we can grasp or recognise. This may be discounted as a subjective reaction to a profoundly moving event, but I do not think I am alone in feeling like this about it.

As you grow older you become more aware that even without the intervention of accident or violence, the time is approaching when the step you have always known to be inevitable is becoming imminent. Mankind is alone in this as in so many other fields. Men and women are the only creatures on the planet who live all their lives in the knowledge of their own death. They are also, so far as we know, the only ones who have ever held any expectation of a life beyond this life.

These matters affect people in different ways. In these days of materialist assumptions, death has become the great unmentionable, the worst thing that can happen to you. The Victorians were great realists about death and covered up sex in a big way. We are just the opposite. Some, perhaps many, rebel at the idea of death. Most people fear it in differing ways, from terror to a mixture of curiosity and apprehension. Many refuse to face it. I have known people unwilling to make their wills because they felt sure that if they did they would die immediately afterwards. Some take a more stoic view and regard any idea of a future life as self-deception, whistling in the dark to keep your courage up. For others any such concept is ruled out by a philosophy of unrelieved materialism, and so they feel that any belief in eternal life is simply a potent wish to prolong the existence of our own ego by rejecting the possibility of its final extinction when we die.

There may be an element of truth in this for all I know, but to me the prospect of eternal life has always seemed more disturbing than quiet extinction,

"GREET THE UNSEEN WITH A CHEER!"

not because of what our forefathers called "hell and damnation" (my father was much against the more highly-coloured, not to say over-heated, expectations in this field) but because of the possibility of being caught up in something from which there is no escape.

Human beings not only live in the expectation of their death: death is, equally, the great escape. If life becomes intolerable, people have always had a way out, irreversible but effective. From eternity, one imagines, there is no way out. The convinced Christian or Muslim doubtless believes nobody would want one. But to think that such a prospect has no anxieties in it is to underestimate the human imagination. Christians, like Muslims, bank on eternal well-being, and I think they are right and that we will find in the paradise of God a mode of existence which we shall eternally enjoy. But since the future remains unknowable except to the eye of faith, there is always, just around the corner out of sight, a lurking anxiety in the mind.

What role this world holds, with its countless millions all down history and in the untold years to come, we have no idea. Prep. school? Proving ground? Source of supply? Long-term experiment? Starting place? The truth is witheld from us. What we can believe is that every human life has its value, and that perhaps there is some accountability, not only for what we have made of our own lives but even more for the effect we have had on others.

There is no evidence that eternal life depends in any way on success or failure in the ordinary meaning of such terms. Ten A-levels will not get you in and lack of any will not keep you out. The test seems to be more, did you care for other people, and how did you live? And even this, I dare say, may be applied more in terms of intention, in the actual circumstances of life, than of any more rigid test of moral performance or religious doctrine. At any rate, this would seem to be the basis on which some of the harlots stand a better chance than some of the more self-righteous Pharisees.

If, as St. Paul held, Christ is "the visible expression of the invisible God", we can afford to trust Him here. We can have confidence that He was able, within the framework of His humanity, to show us enough of the nature of God for us to understand His purposes and to share in what He is doing in our world and beyond it.

If the nature of God is the nature we see in Jesus Christ raised to the unimaginable infinite degree, then at least we know that the Power behind all visible and tangible reality is Love, quick to heal and to forgive, penetrating in His moral clarity, ready to go to any lengths to show His love to man, to us. He is on our side.

In that assurance we can reasonably leave our future in eternity to Him, whatever that eternity may turn out to be.

Perhaps we ought also to give some weight to what some people call the sense of exile. So many people in so many centuries have had this feeling, that on earth we are exiles from our true country, our true mode of existence. Too many have felt this for it to be entirely discounted. "My soul, there is a country, far beyond the stars . . ." We may not feel like Wordsworth that we were born "trailing clouds of glory from Heaven which is our home". But there are those who feel that their lives can never be truly fulfilled till they reach the world to which they really belong. They echo the words of the writer of that potent manifesto rather dauntingly called "The Epistle to the Hebrews": "These all . . . confessed that they were strangers and pilgrims on the earth. For they that say such things declare they seek a country . . . they desire a better country, that is an heavenly. . . ." "They seek a country" – C. S. Lewis called that search the "always aching wound", brought on us by the tyranny of time.

Be that as it may, there is still so much in the human spirit that reaches out to realms that are impossible of attainment here. We do not have the needed powers to paint the pictures, compose the music, write the poetry, build the cities or create the societies which in our deepest being and our ranging imagination we would like to do, and even feel we could do, but circumstances, or our own lack of the needed skills and mental or physical capacity render it impossible, however deeply they may stir us. A few men and women of genius do some of these things for us, in so far as they can, and their pictures and sculptures, their music and poetry, their architecture, their social leadership and their wisdom seem to us to be precious possessions of the whole human race, regardless of what century or what country they come from.

But suppose these inner stirrings in us are in fact radar echoes, foreshadowings of what we are all meant to do on a far richer scale in the dimension which will one day be our true home? Supposing the beauty that pierces us on earth is only a foretaste of beauty at an intensity we cannot now conceive? Here we have never had the talents, most of us, technical or mental or imaginative, or the opportunities and resources to convey what moves most deeply in us. There perhaps all will be possible without limitations of any kind.

All this is speculation. We know so little about the most certain, universal experience of the human race. It is by faith that we must go forward.

"Let not your heart be troubled.... In My Father's house are many mansions.... I go to prepare a place for you."

The deepest truths of our faith come to us in such metaphors. How could it be otherwise? Their images express the inexpressible. How else can you describe what will happen in one dimension for people living in an utterly different one? Yet we have one supreme advantage: in Jesus Christ, God expressed His nature to us in terms we can all comprehend. Clearly in Christ's view, eternal life has already begun for everyone who loves God, whose lives are given to Him. "And this is eternal life, that they might know Thee, the only true God, and Jesus Christ whom Thou hast sent."

We are already part of the comradeship of eternity, with Him and with each other – husband and wife, family, friends. "We know we have passed from death unto life because we love the brethren." And, "because He first loved us".

My father always ended every service he took with this benediction, spoken with great reverence and conviction:

> Now unto Him Who is able to keep us from falling, and to present us faultless before the presence of His glory with exceeding joy, to the only wise God our Saviour, be glory and majesty, dominion and power, now and evermore.